IF AT FIRST...

How Great People Turned Setbacks into Great Success

Laura Fitzgerald

**Andrews McMeel
Publishing**

Kansas City

To Dave,
because without you, I could never have succeeded

IF AT FIRST . . .

ISBN: 0-7407-3835-6

Library of Congress Control Number: 2003064623

04 05 06 07 08 FFG 10 9 8 7 6 5 4 3 2 1

Book design by Holly Camerlinck

Attention: Schools and Businesses
Andrews McMeel books are available at quantity discounts with bulk purchase for
educational, business, or sales promotional use. For information, please write to:
Special Sales Department, Andrews McMeel Publishing, 4520 Main Street,
Kansas City, Missouri 64111.

Contents

Introduction

If you're anything like me, you're a failure.

Oh, sure, you may have a 4.0 GPA and a wall full of degrees and a great job and a killer résumé. But whenever you hit a roadblock on your way to fame and fortune, there's a voice inside you that hisses, "If you fall, you will never get up. If you fail, you are a failure."

Maybe it's because, in our culture, we like to think of people in absolutes: failures or successes. In school, we learn that Edison was the father of the lightbulb—not that he was the father of thousands of failed inventions. Or maybe you learned that Abraham Lincoln made his mark with the Lincoln-Douglas debates. But you probably never learned that he lost the Senate Seat to Douglas. If you're like me, you never learned that behind every great man or woman is the same legacy of setbacks that faces all of us daily—and in many cases, they were setbacks that were greater than anything you've ever imagined.

As you read this book, you'll see that some people rebounded from setbacks less as a deliberate choice and more as a personal philosophy. Winston Churchill's entire career was based on persistence in the face of political reversals. His refusal to give up seemed driven by an internal battle of wills, where to step down from a challenge was tantamount to utter defeat. People like him succeed from sheer perseverance, their one goal to be the last man standing.

Others found in their setbacks a critical moment of decision—an epiphany. If Martin Luther King, Jr., hadn't experienced the failed protests in Albany, Georgia, he might never have learned the necessary lessons that made the Montgomery protests the tipping point for the entire civil rights movement. People like Dr. King transform setbacks into case studies for failure, the basis of new blueprints for success.

Some of the world's greatest heroes might have drifted into personal and political obscurity had it not been for the trials and tribulations that defined them. Would Nelson Mandela be just a country lawyer had he not spent a lifetime of persecution under apartheid? Would the

Dalai Lama be known today as an inconsequential figurehead if the Chinese had not invaded Tibet? With all her senses intact, would Helen Keller have become just another Alabama debutante? It is almost impossible to separate their destinies from the difficult conditions these men and women faced.

And then, in failure, some just got lucky. When Oprah lost her dream job as news anchor, she had no idea that her demotion to talk-show host would be her yellow brick road to success. She was just in the right wrong place at the right wrong time.

Misfortune can be an equal opportunity employer. Many of the people in this book climbed out of poverty using nothing more than their talent and persistence as a ladder. But rich people have setbacks, too. Just look at Eleanor Roosevelt, who, despite a childhood in lavish mansions, never felt at home anywhere. There are successful people like Bernie Marcus, who was a high-flying CEO when he was very publicly fired.

While there are many different people in this book with many different stories and many different approaches, they all have two things in common. They are all great. And they all overcame. What they overcame is, in fact, what often made them great. Setbacks happen to everyone, everywhere, at some time, but what makes great people great is not how or if they fail—it's how they respond when they inevitably do.

And some of those who are truly great even welcome setbacks. They know that the willingness to fail grants them the opportunity to succeed. Just ask Wayne Gretzky: "You miss 100 percent of the shots you don't take." They know that setbacks require them only to work that much harder than the next guy. They know that setbacks give them the opportunity to grow, to transcend themselves, to stumble onto a better way.

So fellow failures, relax and rejoice. For the moral of the story is not that failures can become successful; it's that successful people are failures. And that includes you.

Lance Armstrong

The world's best cyclist fought cancer and came back stronger, faster, and more in love with the sport.

On October 1, 1996, Lance Armstrong was one of the top cyclists in the world. He had won the World Cycling Championships. He had won the U.S. National Road Race Championship with the widest margin in race history. And he had just signed a two-year contract to ride with a prestigious French racing team for $2.5 million.

On October 2, he became a cancer patient.

Earlier that week, he coughed up a sinkful of blood, then found that his testicle had swollen to the size of an orange. A visit to the doctor revealed testicular cancer that had metastasized to the lungs and brain. While emergency surgery was scheduled at once, consulting doctors gave Lance a 50 percent chance for survival—but later admitted they actually pegged it at around 3 percent.

But Lance had never given up easily. Raised by a hardworking single mother in a modest suburban Texas town, he discovered riding early, competing in triathlons at fifteen and winning medals and prize money almost immediately. Biking twenty miles a day to and from swim practice, the route became Lance's way out. "Maybe if I ride my bike on this road long enough," he thought, "it will take me out of here."

Lance was known as a determined, unrelenting rider, a trait he learned from his mother. She once found him near the end of a triathlon exhausted and ready to quit. "Son," she said **"you never quit . . . even if you have to walk."** He finished, walking his way into last place.

For Lance, cancer was just another race—but now, against time. Lance attacked his illness with the same resolve he brought to his bike, undergoing surgery to remove the tumors and then months of chemotherapy. The once invincible cyclist—whose aerobic capacity was the highest on record in research labs around the country—was diminished to a nauseated skeleton, unable to ride his bike even around the neighborhood.

But while the illness had decimated him physically, it had resuscitated him spiritually. Chemo finished and miraculously cancer-free, he slowly returned to training and found that cancer had left him with an unexpected gift: a newfound love for the bike. Until then, his bike had only been "a means to an end . . . a potential source of wealth and recognition." Now it became a symbol of his postcancer mantra, "If I can still move, I'm not sick."

More surprisingly, cancer may actually have eradicated what was holding Lance back—excess weight. Lance had always been known as a superb one-day racer but not to be as competitive in the stage races: multiday and -week races that call for the ability to climb mountainous terrain and that distinguish a world-class rider. He had finished the Tour de France only once, withdrawing due to fatigue and injury in other years. Friends and coaches had told him that he carried too much weight for the steep climbs. Built like a linebacker, Lance believed in muscling his way uphill, ignoring the load he had to drag along.

But postcancer, he stood at 158 pounds, a full 17 pounds lighter than his previous racing weight. And as he climbed the training trails of the Blue Ridge Mountains—and climbed and climbed and climbed–he knew something had changed. He was finally ready to be the best cyclist in the world—in all races, in all terrains, in all conditions.

This revelation carried him to the 1999 Tour de France, where from the initial time trial, he picked up the prized *maillot jaune*, the yellow jersey worn by the leading rider. Although he lost the jersey to other riders halfway through the race, he soon won it back as the race wound its way into the Alps, the site of his earlier defeats. As the race hit its most grueling leg—uphill, through freezing rain—Lance pulled ahead, stretching an overall lead of two minutes and twenty seconds to a full 6:03.

By the time the pack reached its final leg in Paris, Lance rode ahead with an incontestable 7:37 lead. He was met at the finish line by another triumph: his wife, pregnant via in vitro fertilization after Lance's cancer left him sterile.

Lance went on to win the Tour de France again in 2000, 2001, 2002, and 2003, but he wrote: "The truth is, if you asked me to choose between winning the Tour de France and cancer, I would choose cancer . . . because of what it has done for me as a human being, a man, a husband, a son, and a father." In beating cancer, he defeated life's greatest foe: defeat. He rejected doomsday prognoses in favor of hope. He embraced belief—in his courage, in his future, in himself—over doubt.

Lance sums it up best: "I [know] now why people fear cancer: because it is a slow and inevitable death; it *is* the very definition of cynicism and loss of spirit.

"So, I believed."

Oprah Winfrey

She got bounced out of her first big break in television but still landed on her feet.

No one ever accused Oprah Winfrey of taking the easy way out. And yet despite a childhood filled with hardship, the young girl from Kosciusko, Mississippi, always knew that she was destined for greatness.

Maybe it was in this rural backwater that she first learned to "turn your wounds into wisdom," as she would later say. And the wounds were never in short supply. The product of a fling between her mother and a passing serviceman, Oprah was first raised by her grandmother on a pig farm with no running water. She eventually joined her mother, who had moved to Milwaukee, where she experienced the first of many sexual assaults at the hands of family friends and relatives. Oprah retreated into teenage rebellion, and by the time she was fourteen, she had been threatened with juvenile hall and had given birth to a baby boy, who died within a week. Now out of patience, Oprah's mother sent her to live with her father—a man Oprah had never known.

At her father's house, she finally received the discipline she needed to redirect her significant intelligence. Always good in school and well known for her speaking skills, Oprah entered a local beauty pageant, where she won a scholarship to Tennessee State University. She began studying broadcast communications and got a part-time job reporting for a Nashville TV station.

The one-time juvenile delinquent was suddenly unstoppable. Oprah left school to become, at the tender age of nineteen, the first African-American woman to anchor the news in Nashville. Within three years, she was courted and finally won over by a station in Baltimore—a much bigger market with more prestige and exposure. The move would prove to be Oprah's most fortuitous failure.

Oprah's natural poise had always carried her, but now it seemed she'd run out of gas. She forgot to read her copy before she went on the air. She mispronounced "blasé," located Barbados somewhere in California, and chuckled openly at her mistakes. She interviewed a fire victim in classic "How does this make you feel?" fashion, then found herself weeping on the air and apologizing for exploiting the woman's pain.

If the station management was unimpressed with her on-camera conduct, they were downright disgruntled with her looks. They complained that her hair was too thick, her nose too wide, and her eyes too far apart. Attempting to glamorize her image, the station sent Oprah to a chic New York salon that botched a perm so badly, her hair fell out. Unable to find a wig that fit, she went on the air anyway (later saying, "You learn a lot about yourself when you're bald and black and an anchorwoman in Baltimore").

Within a year of Oprah's triumphant arrival, the station had lost interest in their new find. They told her she was unfit for television news. To avoid breaking her contract, they chose not to fire Oprah but instead demoted her from a prime anchor slot to a housewives' daytime talk show, entitled *People Are Talking*.

Oprah has said, **"Failure is really God's way of saying, 'Excuse me, you're moving in the wrong direction.'"** But she was clearly on the right track now. Her first day on the talk show "felt like breathing, which is what your true passion should feel like." The show was a hit with its mostly female audience, too, who saw themselves in this frank, funny, and all-too-human host.

Seven years later, Oprah's show caught the eye of a station in Chicago, where she was invited to move and start A.M. *Chicago*. Within a month, she had grabbed the number one talk-show spot in the market. By 1985, the show was expanded, renamed *The Oprah Winfrey Show,* and nationally syndicated.

Over the next fifteen years of unprecedented success, Oprah continued to share her own particular battles and triumphs within the forum of her show: struggles with food and fat (she finally found *her* weight), a lawsuit brought by cattle ranchers (she won), the "trash TV" programming that dominated her market (she broke free and took the ratings with her). But through it all, she refused to call any of her setbacks mistakes. "I do not believe in failure," Oprah declared. "It isn't failure if you enjoyed the process."

James Earl Jones

The most recognized voice in the world was once silenced by a severe stutter.

It is hard to imagine that the voice of James Earl Jones—the voice of Darth Vader and the lion Mufasa, the voice that greets you when you pick up a Verizon pay phone or turn on CNN, this voice that symbolizes power and authority—was once racked with stops, starts, and repetitions. But as a child, James developed such a debilitating stutter that it was next to impossible to express himself. When other children ridiculed him when he stood up to recite his Bible verses at church, he stopped attending. Soon he refused to speak at all. "I thought, 'If I can't say it, I just won't make an ass of myself,'" James later remembered. "So I didn't talk."

The impediment developed out of childhood trauma. James was the only offspring of a short and unhappy marriage between his mother, a maid and seamstress, and his father, a prize-fighter–turned–actor. James's father left the family shortly after his birth, and with the Depression limiting her ability to work, James's mother turned him over to her parents to raise.

As James, a bright child, reached school age, his grandparents decided to move the family to Michigan in search of a better education and less discrimination. Without sharing their plans with James, they left him with a relative and set off for Michigan, intending to send for him once they were settled on their new farm. Perhaps with his parents' early abandonment fresh in his mind, James assumed he had been left behind. And even though he was put on a train to rejoin his grandparents, James was already traumatized. Soon after he reached Michigan, at the age of five, his family noticed a stutter.

James became functionally mute, remaining silent in public and conducting long conversations with his farm animals, who couldn't pass judgment. Like his great-great-grandfather, he escaped into books, drinking in literary giants and science fiction alike. "I found my voice in books, and I found the expanded vocabulary so important for someone who stutters." This newly discovered voice gave him hours of conversations in his head, while he appeared silent to the outside world. Still, it was a lonely and frustrating existence: "One of the hardest things in life is having words in your heart that you can't utter."

By the time he went off to the local high school, James was acknowledged as a diligent, though exceptionally quiet, student. He got good grades and played basketball and ran track. He did well in his science classes. He reserved a special love for English and his English teacher, Donald Crouch, a retired college professor who assigned all the classics. Jones was particularly taken with *The Song of Hiawatha*, by Henry Wadsworth Longfellow, since it was inspired by the local Chippewa Indian tribe. Asked to bring in a writing assignment to class, James attempted to capture Longfellow's rhythmic language and wrote his own poem, "Ode to a Grapefruit."

Donald Crouch had always suspected great talent lying under James's silent exterior, and the poem gave him an opportunity to test it. Crouch accused James of plagiarizing the poem and insisted he recite it before the class to prove his authorship. James stood in front of the class and recited the poem line by line—and didn't stutter once. Both student and teacher were thrilled with the discovery; it seemed the hidden cure to stuttering was speaking in front of groups.

Enthralled by the new sounds of his own voice, James began to use it wherever he could. He joined the debate team. He became a class officer and editor of the yearbook. He gave poetry readings in front of the entire school, reciting Edgar Allan Poe by candlelight. He even delivered the school's valedictory speech.

James's participation won him a scholarship to the University of Michigan, where, under his grandparents' direction, he began premed studies. But he couldn't stay away from public speaking. He signed up for an acting class to continue working on his speech skills and soon switched his major to drama. He won roles in several campus plays and even Ann Arbor community theater, never once telling teachers or classmates about his stuttering problem. They never guessed.

The path he chose led him to New York City, where he was reunited with his father and introduced to his hero, Paul Robeson, a highly regarded African-American actor and outspoken activist. James did whatever he could to keep taking acting classes: working as a janitor, making sandwiches for a deli, and living in an apartment without heat or electricity. With more acting and speech lessons, James learned not only more about his craft but more about himself. "Because of my muteness, I approached language in a different way from most actors. . . . In those years I spent in virtual silence, I developed a passion for expression, [and] as I regained my power of speech and began to use it as an actor, I came to believe that what is valid about a character is not his intellect, but the sounds he makes."

James's insight and training finally came together at the age of thirty-seven, when he landed his first Broadway role: the lead in a new play, *The Great White Hope*. In the role of a brash young boxer, James won a Tony Award and later won the eye of Hollywood, too, playing the same part in the 1970 movie version, for which he was nominated for an Academy Award.

Today, James Earl Jones is a household name and, more specifically, a household voice. He has been awarded two Tony Awards, four Emmy Awards, a Grammy Award, the National Medal of Arts, and honorary doctorates from Yale, Princeton, and Columbia universities. He has even spoken in front of a congressional committee on literacy to share his testimony about the importance of reading.

Surprisingly, he also still stutters, although much less and not as notice-ably as when he was a child. But James knows how much he owes to that affliction. It has spurred him to a more intimate relationship with language and a deeper understanding of himself and his characters. More important, it has given him an obstacle that he must overcome daily, constantly challenging himself to find meaning and knowledge in his burden. Perhaps this is why he charged recent college graduates with the challenge: "So let us dream; let us hope and pray; **let us reinvent ourselves every morning.**"

Eleanor Roosevelt

A "poor little rich girl" becomes America's best-loved First Lady and the world's best-known humanitarian.

Born into a family of means, Anna Eleanor Roosevelt seemed an unlikely candidate for a hard-luck story. As the daughter of New York socialites, Eleanor grew up in an extremely wealthy and privileged home. Eleanor's connections began with her uncle President Theodore Roosevelt and continued through her parents: an immensely popular playboy and big-game hunter, and one of the most beautiful debutantes in New York.

But Eleanor was painfully shy, physically gawky, and socially awkward. She was largely ignored by her mother, who was disappointed with Eleanor's plainness and lack of grace, calling her "Granny" in front of guests. Eleanor was only eight when her mother died of diphtheria, but she was at least able to lean on her father. She idolized the fun-loving man who was affectionate and attentive—when he was able. An alcoholic, he once told the nine-year-old Eleanor to wait for him outside a men's club while he had a quick drink. Six hours later, she watched as he was carried out, unconscious, by the club's porters, who sent him home in a cab. He was ultimately banished from home and drank himself to death shortly thereafter.

The young Eleanor went to live with her grandmother, where life was slightly more stable but no more comforting. No play was allowed, and Eleanor was expected to be seen and not heard. Her aunts, uncles, and cousins—some of whom were also alcoholics—had no time for her. Because of the general sense of gloom around the house, no friends wanted to visit, and Eleanor wasn't able to adapt to the social scene as she reached adolescence. Since restrictive Victorian rules limited her movement, Eleanor had no escape. She was trapped in the margins of her own life, feeling like an outsider in her peer group and in her own family.

Boarding school provided Eleanor with one brief and shining respite from her dreary childhood. Her headmaster saw Eleanor's potential, and under her tutelage, Eleanor became the prized pet of the school, loved by teachers and students alike. For three short years, she blossomed, speaking up in class, leading organizations, and even playing varsity sports. But this golden era was cut short by Eleanor's grandmother, who summoned her back to New York at eighteen to make her debut in society. Eleanor feared and hated the entire process. All too aware that she was the first girl in her family not to become the year's favorite debutante, she left the ball early. She did, however, continue to make the obligatory social rounds, where she was usually seated next to older guests at dinner parties, since she was known for her maturity and good conversation.

All the year's debutantes were enrolled in the Junior League, a society women's organization that strove to champion social causes. Eleanor found her niche there, disdaining the fund-raising parties most girls volunteered for and immersing herself in the dirty work. At a time when women were not supposed to leave their social circles, Eleanor would travel to the slums of the Lower East Side of New York City to teach classes at a settlement house for immigrant girls. Intrigued by the working lives of these girls, she then joined the Consumer's League, which visited sweatshops to observe the working conditions. Eleanor was horrified to see women working fourteen-hour days alongside children as young as four. There was something about these immigrants' marginalization that spoke to her and with which she identified.

Fortunately, she was able to share the experience with a new friend. She had met her fifth cousin Franklin Delano Roosevelt on her social rounds and invited the gallant Harvard student to accompany her on her volunteer calls. Franklin became smitten with Eleanor's sharp mind and tender heart. He was also profoundly moved by the poverty he observed. It was an experience that he would carry with him all the way to the White House; this would not be the last time Eleanor introduced Franklin to a worthy cause or an unobserved plight.

Eleanor and Franklin's marriage finally brought her into close contact with an intellectual equal, but she felt smothered by her new role of wife and mother. Once married, she found her options again heavily restricted. The role of mother to five children did not come easily to Eleanor, given her lack of positive parental role models. She suffered from depressive episodes. Franklin's domineering mother made all the couple's decisions, even commissioning adjoining townhouses in New York with connecting doors on every floor. Eleanor feared that she was "simply absorbing the personalities of those about me and letting their tastes and interests dominate me," for when she wasn't acquiescing to her mother-in-law, she was submitting to her husband. This made the news of his affair with her social secretary that much more difficult to stand. She offered Franklin a divorce, and while he refused and tried to patch up their marriage, their relationship became largely a political partnership from that time on.

It was a partnership that met its greatest challenge when Franklin contracted polio. Paralyzed from the waist down, he was forced to briefly give up a burgeoning political career and spend most of his time in rehabilitation. Besides nursing her sick husband, Eleanor was obliged to take over Franklin's role as family leader. She became both mother and father to her children, learning to swim so she could teach them and taking the boys on camping trips in the Canadian wilderness. She also began standing up to her mother-in-law, who insisted on taking over Franklin's care herself.

Later in life, when Eleanor encouraged others, **"You must do the thing you think you cannot do,"** she must have reflected on this turning point. For what Franklin most needed were Eleanor's efforts outside the family as an active lobbyist for his political aspirations. After having accompanied her husband on the campaign trail, and after some successes as a wartime volunteer for the Red Cross and the League of Women Voters, she tentatively dipped her toe in the political waters. Once shocked by the idea of woman suffrage, she now joined the women's division of the New York State Democratic Party, where she soon overcame her innate shyness to speak to groups and organize new women's chapters. Remembering her days on the Lower East Side, she became involved in labor concerns and lobbied for shorter workweeks and an end to child labor. She gave interviews and wrote for newspapers and magazines, and soon the Roosevelt name was tied to progressive causes. Eleanor wrote that Franklin's polio attack "proved to be a blessing in disguise, for it gave him strength and courage he had not had before." She might as well have been writing it about herself.

Her efforts sustained Franklin's campaign until he was fit enough to run for governor. After winning, then being reelected by the state's largest margin ever, a presidential run was a matter of course and Franklin's win inevitable. Eleanor feared the move to the White House; now that she had gotten a taste of her own abilities, she did not want to lose her freedom to speak out and act. But just as she had as the governor's wife, she became Franklin's closest adviser—his eyes, ears, and legs, traveling across the country and around the world to bear witness to what Franklin could not.

Because of her constant travel, she gained the name "Everywhere Eleanor." She wrote a daily newspaper column, held press conferences for an all-female press corps, and lectured throughout the country. She traveled to see Puerto Rican slums, Appalachian coal miners, and Deep South sharecroppers. When World War II broke out, she flew on an army bomber to see soldiers in some of the most dangerous sites in the Pacific theater, wearing her Red Cross uniform to visit with the wounded boys.

Even without her husband's open support, Eleanor became the era's most prominent civil rights advocate, denouncing discrimination and flaunting segregation laws on her visit to the South. When the Daughters of the American Revolution refused to allow the black opera singer Marian Anderson to perform in their auditorium, Mrs. Roosevelt publicly resigned from the organization. She then organized a free concert on the steps of the Lincoln Memorial, which was attended by 75,000 people. A legacy of her own alienated childhood, she continued to identify with the country's outsiders—the poor, the unemployed, the persecuted—and strove to make concrete changes in their daily lives. The New Deal could even be construed as her need to take care of the neglected on a national scale.

Eleanor continued to advise the country's presidents even after Franklin's death. President Truman acknowledged her humanitarian triumphs by appointing her to the U.S. delegation to the United Nations. As the chair of the U.N. Commission on Human Rights, she helped shape the Universal Declaration of Human Rights, a document that is to this day the most widely recognized and adopted civil rights statement in the world. By the time Mrs. Roosevelt died in 1962, she had been voted the most admired woman in America for eleven years in a row. It is an honor unmatched to this day.

Michael Jordan

His greatest childhood defeat spurred him through a lifetime of athletic dominance.

When spectators watch Michael Jordan play, they don't just see a man who has redefined athletic achievement for our time but a fierce competitor for whom every game becomes a battle of wills. And while he is known for an unprecedented winning record, it has always been failure that has spurred Michael to his greatest effort: "I know fear is an obstacle for some people, but it is an illusion to me. . . . Failure always made me try harder next time."

Michael came by his competitive streak naturally. One of five children in a disciplined and driven family, he was raised with high standards and higher expectations. Once after he skipped school, Michael's mother took him to work and made him sit in the car studying all day while she watched him from her office window. The family saw that Michael excelled not only in school, but also in his extracurricular activities. His first taste of athletic excellence came on his Little League team, where he was known for pitching no-hitters. But basketball prowess was just a dream; at five feet eight inches, he was too short to prove much of a threat on the court.

But he loved the game, and his passion and competitive drive were fueled by his ongoing rivalry with his brother Larry. The two faced off in epic bouts of one-on-one in their backyard every day, with Larry usually dominating his younger brother. In fact, Larry was considered to be the true athlete in the family by his siblings and his high school coaches, who later speculated that Michael might have become known as "Larry's brother" had Larry ever grown taller than five feet seven inches. Michael hated losing—to his brother or to anyone else—and friends and family remember that he would continue challenging them to game after game of Horse until he finally won. But he later admitted his debt to his older brother: "When you see me play, you see Larry play."

The local high school coaches knew of Michael through Larry and invited him to their summer basketball camp before he started high school. He, along with one of his best friends, was asked to try out for the varsity team. Michael impressed everyone at the camp with his speed and dexterity, but the coaches were worried that he hadn't hit his growth spurt and thought he might do well to play on the junior varsity team for a year to get more court time. When the varsity roster was finally posted, Michael's friend—all six feet six inches of him—was there on the list. But Michael wasn't.

It was a defining moment of Michael's life. He stared at the alphabetical list, rereading the Js over and over again, convinced his coach had made a mistake. He later confessed that he went home and cried that day, overwhelmed by feelings of disappointment and embarrassment. Fortunately, his mother was there for Michael with some important advice: "[She] said the best thing for me to do was to prove to the coach that he was wrong," Michael later remembered. "And I started working on my game the day after I was cut."

Michael reluctantly joined the junior varsity squad. But while he had always been known as a dedicated player, he stepped up his training with a new intensity. Michael's PE teacher, Ruby Sutton, saw the change firsthand: "I normally get to school between seven and seven-thirty. Michael would be at school before I would. Every time I'd come in and open these doors, I'd hear the basketball. Fall, wintertime, summertime. Most mornings, I had to run Michael out of the gym." Since it was his height that kept him off the varsity team, Michael even tried hanging from a chin-up bar to stretch out his body an extra inch.

Even without the six-foot frame, Michael quickly became the junior varsity's star player. His speed and skill were unmatched by his teammates. Before long, the varsity team began showing up early to games just to watch Michael lead the JV, scoring twenty-five and sometimes even forty points a game. The JV improved as a team, since Michael demanded the same intensity from his teammates as he did from himself, egging his coaches on to push the team harder when they bristled under his criticism. At the end of the day, his assistant coach, Fred Lynch, said, Michael was a "sore loser. . . . What he always expected was everybody play the game as hard as he played it."

By the beginning of his junior year, Michael had grown four inches. His large hands gave him better reach and grip, and now he could dunk. The coaches were pleased with his newfound height, and they could no longer ignore his talent. When he was finally tapped to join the varsity team, he brought with him something that would inspire every coach, teammate, and fan for the rest of his career: an unmatched level of skill made possible by unmatchable drive and commitment.

And behind Michael Jordan's skill and drive lay his secret: an enduring respect for failure that allowed him to harness it to his advantage. Years later, Michael motivated himself by returning to that original setback:

"Whenever I was working out and got tired and figured I ought to stop, I'd close my eyes and see that list in the locker room without my name on it, and that usually got me going again." In fact, for a man who became the most celebrated and acclaimed player in the history of the game—with six NBA championships, five MVP awards, twelve All-Star games, an NCAA title, and two Olympic gold medals—Michael knew that he succeeded only because of his willingness to fail. **"I can accept failure. Everyone fails at something. But I can't accept not trying."**

Mohandas Gandhi

The man who stood up to the British Empire had to first stand up to his own personal shortcomings.

Perhaps the only thing more surprising than Gandhi's extraordinary leadership, eloquence, and inner strength was his childhood—which, by all accounts, was a disappointment to all who knew him. It was only after many years of unrelenting defeats that he could write, **"If you are afraid of committing a mistake, you are afraid of doing anything at all."**

Born Mohandas Karamchand Gandhi, the young "Mahatma" ("Great-Souled") was considered unspectacular in every way: a middling student with no discernible talents or gifts and the youngest son of a midranking caste family of civil servants from a small seaside Indian town. Keeping with local traditions, he was married off at the age of thirteen to a family friend's daughter, who found him impatient, jealous, and domineering.

His unpleasant manner stemmed from his crippling shyness and utter lack of confidence. He ran home from school every day as soon as classes ended, terrified of speaking to his classmates lest they make fun of him. In fact, he was overwhelmed by irrational fears of all kinds and slept with a light on through his teens to keep away visions of snakes, thieves, and ghosts.

Barely graduating from high school, he dutifully went on to the local college with a vague ambition of becoming a doctor. He then proceeded to fail every class and to return home in disgrace after only five months.

With an apparently hopeless case on their hands, Gandhi's family pooled their contacts and resources. They finally decided to send him to England to study for a barrister's license—a path that ensured some level of success without requiring great intellectual ability. Gandhi looked forward to the fresh start and shopped carefully for dapper European clothes to help him fit into his new environment. When he arrived in London, he found himself a laughingstock—stumbling through his schoolbook English and sticking out in white summer flannels in the middle of autumn.

Undaunted, he applied himself diligently to his studies. He rapidly tried to out-British the Brits, buying all suits and taking up French, dancing, violin, and elocution lessons. But he soon found that his limited funds couldn't support these extravagances, and before long, he abandoned his hotel for a small room of his own. He started covering all of London on foot to save on bus fare and traded heavy English food for a spare vegetarian diet. Ironically, these early economies would later become cornerstones of his teachings on health and simplicity.

The day after Gandhi passed his exams and was appointed to the bar, he sailed home to India, only to find that his mother had died during his passage. He staved off his grief by moving again, this time to Bombay, where he tried to establish himself as a lawyer. But his formal training in London left him completely unqualified to deal with the realities of Indian law. When he finally secured a case—a simple ten-dollar claim—he found that he was too afraid to perform the cross-examination. Trembling, with his voice caught in his throat, he handed the brief to a more experienced colleague and fled the courtroom without a word, the laughter of the court ringing in his ears.

Again Gandhi returned home in failure, and again his family came to his rescue. This time a brother used his connections to secure Gandhi a low-ranking desk job with a firm in South Africa. With no other opportunities in sight, he set sail, leaving his wife and two sons behind after less than two years at home.

True to form, Gandhi arrived in South Africa to find himself in over his head. There was no clerical job awaiting him, but rather a position requiring a highly skilled bookkeeper who could decipher years of complicated business transactions for an intricate and contentious legal case. It seemed that no matter where Gandhi jumped, he seemed destined to fall on his face.

But not this time. He took a long, hard look at the challenge ahead. It did not escape him that his luck stayed the same despite the many ways he changed his environment. The one constant, he observed, was himself. If he could change his position, his location, his situation—why couldn't he change himself? It was a revolutionary thought for the struggling clerk. What he did not yet realize was that it would prove to be revolutionary for his people as well.

Gandhi began studying the details of the case and the perplexities of bookkeeping with a newfound passion. He surprised himself with his own competency and became respected as the most knowledgeable lawyer on the case. More important, he began to question the antagonistic, even punitive, nature of the lawsuit, a dispute between blood relatives that had escalated into a full-blown feud. He rejected the dictate to pursue only the interests of his client and set about finding a just resolution—and ultimately reconciliation—for both parties. In the end, he persuaded both sides to settle out of court.

He later wrote: "I had learnt the true practice of law. I had learnt to find out the better side of human nature and enter men's hearts."

This revelation became the root of Gandhi's life philosophy. It would drive him to demand meetings with British leaders and work with them as equals; to find common ground with members of all castes, religions, and nationalities; to insist on independence for his country and on the highest standards for his people. His work for civil rights and Indian independence and his enduring belief in love and nonviolence stemmed from this idea: that all people can be transformed, that all people can change from within, that all people are capable of the same powerful action in the name of what's good.

Helen Keller

Deaf and blind, her greatest miracle was her belief that she— and all the disabled—should simply be treated as people.

The story of Helen Keller has entered into American legend. Even schoolchildren know the story of Helen's release from silent isolation at the family water pump, as dramatized on stage and screen in *The Miracle Worker*. But Helen's greatest fight began where the story ends. As she would discover, her greatest challenge wasn't learning to communicate; it was her lifelong fight to be fully accepted as a human being, no matter what her disability.

Helen Keller was an alert and vivacious baby. Her parents, wealthy landowners in post–Civil War Alabama, boasted of signs of her innate intelligence, even claiming she spoke her first words, "How do you do?" at six months. But after she was struck by scarlet fever at nineteen months, her parents could not ignore the change in her. Bright light hurt her eyes, then after a few days, she didn't respond to light or shapes at all. It soon became clear that the toddler had lost her hearing in addition to her sight, and as she became further engulfed by her own silence, she lost her speech as well.

Cut off from her parents' words, both kind and stern, Helen became a virtual savage. With no way to express her frustration, she flew into wild fits and attacks when she didn't get her way, which only became worse as her parents became more and more reluctant to discipline her. Well-meaning relatives saw no alternative: commit the girl to a mental institution, where she would be tended to as if she were mentally disabled or insane.

Still, the mute child did not seem to be mentally deficient. By the age of five, she had invented her own system of sign language, consisting of sixty gestures, including "Mother," "Father," "bread," and "candy." Believing Helen could be educated, her mother took her to see Alexander Graham Bell, who was working with the deaf at the time. Through a series of recommendations, a young graduate of the Perkins School for the Blind in Boston, Annie Sullivan, was arranged to travel south as Helen's private tutor.

Annie saw in Helen what no one else could: a little girl, just like any other. She refused to coddle her or excuse her bad behavior. She disciplined her strictly, even teaching Helen in one afternoon to sit and eat with a fork, after a lifetime of grabbing food off others' plates. Annie didn't always win, though; within the first week of working with Helen, she had lost her two front teeth.

Annie showed Helen sign language, spelling individual letters into the girl's hand. Helen, starved for mental stimulation, picked up quickly on what she considered a game and memorized one letter combination after another. But she did not seem to understand that these combinations made up words, and that these words had meanings that corresponded to objects and ideas. It was simply an elaborate game like Rock, Paper, Scissors.

Not until Annie held Helen's hand under a running water pump and continuously spelled out "water" did Helen understand. She finally grasped that w-a-t-e-r was what she once called "wa-wa" before the fever, and this w-a-t-e-r was that cold, wet, splashing thing in her hands. Language was the escape from her dark, silent isolation, and she raced to learn more words. By the end of the day, she knew 30. In another three months, she knew 300.

Friends, family, and neighbors were staggered by the transformation, and news of Helen's accomplishments spread across the country. When she revisited Alexander Graham Bell the following year, he remarked, "Her achievement is without parallel in the education of the deaf." The trip was followed by a visit with President Grover Cleveland. By the age of twelve, Helen was world-famous, counting Mark Twain, John D. Rockefeller, Andrew Carnegie, England's Queen Victoria, and Queen Olga of Greece as admirers.

Helen was hailed for her achievements far and wide, yet despite her hard work and fighting spirit, some still viewed her as feeble and weak. Helen rejected this label; in fact, her disabilities became her source of strength: "I thank God for my handicaps, for, through them, I have found myself, my work, and my God." When both she and Annie realized that Helen needed more education than Annie could provide alone, they arranged for her to go to the Perkins School for the Blind, where Annie had been schooled, to spend several winters. Here Helen mastered work not only in her own language, but also in French, Greek, and Latin. And when dreams of college beckoned, she continued her high school studies in Cambridge so she could study near her dream school, Radcliffe, the sister college to Harvard.

At school in Cambridge, Helen threw herself into her studies with the same enthusiasm and even more hard work, since this school had no facilities for the deaf or blind. With Annie by her side, Helen diligently prepared for her entrance exams. But the headmaster worried that the girl was not up to the challenge. He accused Annie of pushing her too hard and not taking Helen's disabilities seriously. What Helen needed, he reasoned, was to slow down and set her expectations a bit lower. When Annie protested, he forcibly separated the two and wrote Helen's mother that Annie was recklessly endangering her daughter's health. Mrs. Keller hurried to Cambridge to assess the situation and listening to Helen's demands, withdrew her from the school and reunited her with Annie. Helen undertook the rest of her preparation under independent study but with the same hard work.

Helen was further disappointed with her treatment at Radcliffe. After passing the entrance exams and receiving especially high marks on her Latin exam, the dean of admissions met with her privately. Once again, a school was worried that the curriculum would prove to be too difficult for a blind and deaf student. They would hate to see Helen work twice as hard as the other students only to ultimately fail. They declined Helen's admission to the class of 1899.

Helen was devastated but determined. When Cornell University and the University of Chicago admitted her and awarded substantial scholarships, she turned them down and set to work studying for Radcliffe's next set of entrance exams. The next year brought another set of high scores and Helen's entry into the class of 1900. She not only graduated with honors, but also wrote her memoir, *The Story of My Life,* while pursuing a full class load. The book went on to become a critically acclaimed and worldwide best-seller.

Helen spent the rest of her life fighting to take on the challenges available to any other able person, insisting, **"Life is either a daring adventure or nothing."** She learned to swim, to ride a bicycle, to ride a horse, and to camp. She took controversial political stances, openly aligning herself with woman suffrage, pacifism, and socialism even though she was advised to keep quiet. When money became tight, she and Annie took to the vaudeville stage, which Helen's relatives thought vulgar, with an extremely popular question-and-answer routine meant to educate even common Americans on her struggle.

When Annie's sight became too weak to be of help to her charge, Helen rededicated herself to the rights of the disabled. She refused publishers' offers to write more and more memoirs and traveled and spoke instead to raise money for the American Foundation for the Blind. Through these efforts, she traveled around the world, meeting

Albert Einstein, Winston Churchill, the emperor of Japan, and every American president of her lifetime. Through her personal example and public appearances, Helen Keller did more to change the perception, education, and treatment of the disabled around the world than any other activist.

After Annie's death, Helen wrote her friend's biography, but the nearly completed manuscript was lost in a fire in 1946. In a final testament to Annie's tenacity, Helen started again from scratch. She published *Teacher: Annie Sullivan Macy* in 1955. Thirteen years later, Helen was buried next to her friend and teacher at the National Cathedral in Washington, D.C.

Jimmy Carter

A discounted and defeated president became the world's moral leader by rededicating himself to his personal beliefs.

Nine A.M., January 20, 1981. In the final hours of his presidency, Jimmy Carter waited in the Oval Office. He had sat up all night by the phone, waiting for a call that never came, a call announcing that the fifty-two hostages being held in Iran were free. Jimmy had been devastated when workers in the American embassy were seized, and while all his efforts to secure their freedom had been futile, he had assurances that the Iranian government would help make this one act his final legacy. Iran did release the hostages—at 12:01 P.M., exactly one minute after Ronald Reagan was sworn in as America's new president.

It was the final blow in a disappointing and defeated presidency, and it was hard to remember that just four years earlier, Jimmy Carter had been considered America's great hope. When the peanut farmer from Plains, Georgia (population 600), began his campaign, he was unknown to anyone outside his home state, and with only three years under his belt as governor, he was even a stranger to some there. But with persistent campaigning from coast to coast, his quiet, earnest determination and aw-shucks manner finally won over a nation—just barely. Carter narrowly beat incumbent Gerald Ford at the polls in one of the closest presidential races in history.

When Jimmy entered office in 1977, he was seen as a necessary breath of fresh air that would blow out the lingering stench of Watergate corruption. He had run largely on a character platform, leaving the issues to concentrate on his impeccable ethical record. A Great Depression baby, devout Southern Baptist, and small-town farmer, he brought his own values of thrift and hard work to the job. But while these values won votes on the campaign trail, they alienated most Americans when preached from the White House. Sitting by a fire and wearing a cardigan sweater, he implored his fellow citizens to help fight the energy crisis by turning down their thermostats to sixty-five degrees. Americans were not won over, even as they waited in long lines at the gas station. In most people's minds, Carter was to blame for the crisis.

No one would argue that Jimmy Carter didn't know how to get things done. He had an impressive record when it came to foreign policy—brokering the SALT II arms control treaty with the Soviet Union, giving more attention to African nationalism than any other president, and, most important, engineering the Camp David accords, which achieved a lasting peace between Egypt and Israel.

But at home, it seemed Jimmy couldn't pass even the simplest bill. He lost support from Democrats and Republicans alike by slashing fat from budgets and proposals, and they responded by tying up his bills in congressional committee. Fellow politicians labeled him a stubborn do-gooder. A politician from Georgia summed it up best, calling him a "turtle who's been blocked by a log—he just keeps pushing, pushing, pushing, straight ahead."

And as his political foundation crumbled, the world's events conspired to speed the demolition. Iranian students following the Ayatollah Khomeini took American workers hostage at the U.S. embassy, and the economy worsened in the grip of the growing energy crisis. The Soviet Union invaded Afghanistan, and Jimmy lost more support nationwide when he protested by refusing to send the U.S. Olympic Team to the 1980 Moscow games.

Mired in the overwhelming tide of events and his own ineffectiveness, Jimmy Carter labored to revive his reputation but was defeated soundly by Ronald Reagan in the 1980 election. The former president left Washington to return to Plains, Georgia, site of his childhood dreams and his first run for state senate. Facing what he feared would be "an altogether new, unwanted, and potentially empty life," he embarked on the activities of an ex-president: writing his memoirs, teaching, and speaking.

Jimmy also could not help but reflect on his religious faith and the failure that had brought him to it. Fifteen years earlier, he had gone through a similar depression when he ran for governor of Georgia and lost. Despondent, the lifelong churchgoer had renewed his spiritual commitment, becoming "born again" in his relationship with Christ. His religious faith sustained him through another run for governor, which he won this time. In office, he put his beliefs into practice, promising in his inaugural address that "the time for racial discrimination is over," and including more blacks and women in his administration than any governor before him.

Now, with the presidency and any political ambitions in his past, Carter returned again to his spiritual base. He continued attending the local Baptist church in Plains and became aware of a new organization just nine miles away, dedicated to building homes for the poor. The group, Habitat for Humanity, was founded around a strong Christian philosophy that complemented Jimmy's own concerns for the poor and marginalized. A carpenter by hobby, he began contributing his time and money to the organization, even being featured on the front page of the *New York Times* as he stepped off a Trailways bus and went to work on a house in Harlem. Today, he has become virtually indistinguishable from the public face of Habitat.

The success of Habitat brought the former president back to an old saying of his: **"You can do what you have to do, and sometimes you can do it even better than you think you can."** He began to reflect on his own successes. While his presidency was remembered chiefly as one filled with failures, Carter built on the area where he had the most impact: foreign policy and, more specifically, his dedication to human rights and peacemaking. He and his wife, Rosalynn, created the Carter Center, a not-for-profit organization that strives to spread peace and democracy while fighting the plights of the poor: hunger, disease, and poverty. That "turtle" has applied his particularly insistent morality and gained international attention for mediating multiparty elections, seeking peaceful solutions to civil conflicts, and supporting fair economic development and human rights. The center has been instrumental in fighting preventable diseases, most notably in the near-eradication of Guinea worm disease in African countries that have largely been ignored by the developed world.

In 2002, Jimmy Carter won the Nobel Peace Prize for his work with the Carter Center. He has been called "the only man who's ever used the presidency as a stepping-stone to greater things" and is widely considered the most successful and effective ex-president in history. More than two decades after his humiliating defeat, Jimmy Carter's efforts have paid off, not just for the thousands of people who have benefited from his dedication, but for his own role in history and the very definition of the position of ex-president.

Anita Roddick

**Necessity uncovered the business insight that drove
The Body Shop to success.**

Not many women would cheerfully encourage their husbands to leave on a two-year expedition while they stayed at home supporting two young children. But then Anita Roddick had never been like other women.

Anita's earliest memories were of working in her parents' café in the English seaside town of Littlehampton. The daughter of two Italian immigrants, she was quickly absorbed into their work ethic, which she later likened to "legitimate child labor." She thought nothing of working her weekends in the café, then sleeping in one room with her extended family while the other rooms in their house were rented out to boarders.

As part of an immigrant group in a homogeneous seaside town, Anita identified early with outsiders. At age ten, a book on the Holocaust made a lasting impression and awakened her interest in human rights and justice. She trained at a teachers college and began teaching in public schools, but a scholarship to teach on a kibbutz in Israel launched a lifelong love of travel and other cultures.

Her time on the kibbutz ended abruptly when Anita was fired for her role in a juvenile prank. While a blow for her teaching credentials, the incident cut Anita loose from the responsibility that had tied her to work her whole life. She traveled home the long way, hitchhiking around Israel and living in Paris and Switzerland for a spell. She eventually left teaching for good and spent a year traveling to Tahiti, New Caledonia, Australia, Madagascar, and finally South Africa, where she was expelled from the country for visiting a jazz club on "black night."

Out of money and homesick, she returned to England and fell in love with Gordon Roddick, a young writer and poet who frequented her mother's café-turned-bar. Within two years, they were married with one daughter and another on the way. Gordon tried to support the family with a picture-framing shop, but when that went under, he and Anita went into business together, buying a ramshackle eight-room bed-and-breakfast. Although they spent weeks transforming it into a viable business, the lack of visitors to their sleepy town forced them to turn it into a boardinghouse.

Looking for another income stream, Anita and Gordon became besotted with a restaurant space and, drawing on Anita's childhood experience, decided to open a café. Paddington's Restaurant opened with a gourmet health-food menu, £10,000 in bank loans—and a local clientele who had never heard of quiche. Nor were the locals very interested. For the first month, the restaurant sat empty. On the brink of bankruptcy, Gordon ran out and bought a grill and fryer and began turning out steaks, hamburgers, and English chips. The business took off.

For three years, the restaurant was the most popular fry-shop in town. But three years of coming home from the restaurant at 1 A.M. and getting up early to run a boardinghouse were too much for the Roddicks, especially as they were only breaking even. They worried, too, that their two daughters were growing closer to their grandmother who looked after them than to their own parents.

And Gordon had his own reasons for packing it in. He was ready to pursue his childhood dream: following in the footsteps of a famous Swiss explorer by riding horseback 5,300 miles from Buenos Aires to New York. To his surprise, his travel-loving wife endorsed the trip wholeheartedly. They sold the restaurant and the boardinghouse and looked for a small business idea that would support the family in Gordon's absence but allow Anita to work nine to five and still be home with the children at night.

Anita's idea—a cosmetics shop using all the natural ingredients she'd encountered on her world travels—was a hard sell to the bank, which refused to give her a loan when she showed up in a Bob Dylan shirt and jeans, with two children on her hip. Gordon went back to the bank with her, having forced Anita into a conservative business suit and having typed out an impressive business plan bound in a folder. Anita was infuriated but relieved when the bank handed over a check for £4,000 immediately, which she used to buy raw ingredients and to rent a small retail space in nearby artsy Brighton.

With no training or experience, Anita opened The Body Shop in 1976 with only fifteen products. Annoyed for years that she couldn't find small or sample sizes of her favorite cosmetics, the store featured five different sizes of each product—although she later admitted that this was also prompted by a need to make the sparse store shelves seem packed with offerings.

Many of The Body Shop's environmentally conscious policies were the result of such economic necessity. Anita later wrote, "I made no claim to prescience, to any intuition about the rise of the green movement. **At the forefront of my mind at that time, there was really only one thought—survival."** When the store opened, Anita invested in the cheapest bottles she could find for her lotions and potions—the plastic kind used by hospitals to collect urine samples. And since she didn't have enough money to secure enough of even these, she started the store's practice of refilling customers' bottles, a policy that found supporters among the town's green-friendly artists and thrifty World War II generation alike. And while the store's signature dark green walls came to symbolize the company's commitment to recycling and sustainability, Anita originally chose the color to cover the shop's unsightly water stains.

Anita even turned a last-ditch effort to keep the shop from opening into a PR event. When two nearby funeral parlors initiated a lawsuit claiming the name "The Body Shop" would hurt their businesses, Anita called in an anonymous tip to the local paper, who covered the situation as a human interest story a week before the store opened. Gordon had advised Anita before leaving that if she couldn't make £300 a week with the store, she should close it down and join him in South America. On The Body Shop's opening day, she made £130. Anita decided then and there never to pay for advertising as long as she owned the store.

By the time Gordon returned home, Anita had opened a second Body Shop in a neighboring town. Gordon was impressed and suggested a plan for "self-financing" more shops. Together they began selling franchises to interested buyers. They used the capital raised to expand their product range. By 1982, the couple was opening new stores at the rate of two a month. In 1984, The Body Shop went public.

Besides establishing itself as a major force in skin and body care, The Body Shop had transformed itself from just a cosmetics store to a platform for political activism. The new publicly held company was launched with an overt mission: "to dedicate our business to the pursuit of social and environmental change." The company was one of the first big businesses to come out against animal testing, and its store windows have been as likely to promote the benefits of fair trade and high self-esteem as shea butter and tea tree oil.

Today, the store in Brighton has become over 2,000 stores in more than 50 countries. The original 15 products now number over 600. The woman who was once denied a bank loan has helped launch a university business degree course and has been honored with knighthood, accepting the title of DBE (Dame Commander of the Order of the British Empire). The remarkable young woman who defied expectations has become a remarkable older woman with the same goals. Although Anita stepped down from a managing role in 2002, she continues to advise the company creatively and to promote the many causes that provoke her. She finds particular inspiration in the quote "A woman in advancing old age is unstoppable by any earthly force." Then again, being unstoppable is something Anita perfected a long time ago.

George Washington Carver

Born into slavery, George Washington Carver overcame his own poverty to help struggling black and white farmers alike.

When George Washington Carver arrived at Highland College for his freshman year, he brought with him a certain amount of self-confidence. Growing up, he was accustomed to changing schools whenever he found he knew more than the teachers, and his college application had showcased his impeccable grades and recommendations. But when he went to register for classes, the administration turned him away and rescinded their offer. They had assumed from his application that he was white.

Born into slavery near the beginning of the Civil War, George had been kidnapped along with his mother by slave raiders when he was only a baby. While George's mother was sold and sent away, George's owner was able to get him back in exchange for a prized racehorse. His owners then raised George and his brother as their own sons, and their neighbors came to accept them as members of the family.

Too sickly and weak to work the farm like his brother, George was often kept inside to help his foster mother with the chores and to pursue his studies. To keep him busy, he was given responsibility for the family garden, which he tended with great devotion and scientific interest. He became known far and wide as the "plant doctor" for his ability to resuscitate even the most decrepit plant. What little free time he had, George spent wandering the woods, inspecting every tree, shrub, insect, and woodland creature he could find. He brought home for observation whatever he could fit into his pockets.

So when George found himself demoralized and rejected by Highland College, he left his education behind and returned to the prairie to try his luck as a homesteader. But the knowledge gleaned from a farmland upbringing was not enough to overcome the property's shortcomings. His plot—bought sight unseen—had no water, and George was forced to traipse back and forth between the farm and a neighbor's property, hauling water for his crops. The winters were brutal with blizzards. The summers were blazing with constant drought. Not even the "plant doctor" could save these crops. Whatever he was able to grow could not cover his debts, and he eventually surrendered the land to his creditors. But the hardships he bore on the prairie would later serve as the launching point for his most important work.

George made a last-ditch effort to continue his education and became the first black student admitted to Iowa's Simpson College. The small school appealed to him for its art program, and he enthusiastically enrolled and began pursuing his favorite pastime: painting flowers. His paintings caught the eye of a horticulture professor, who, amazed by George's discerning eye for detail, convinced the young man that perhaps scientific study was his true calling. George soon transferred to Iowa State Agricultural College, where he would earn bachelor's and master's degrees. He became the first African American appointed to the faculty—all the while working odd jobs as a janitor, cook, and launderer to pay his own way.

The news of George's success traveled in academic circles and caught the attention of Booker T. Washington, who had founded the Tuskegee Normal and Industrial Institute, a school in Alabama dedicated to vocational training for African Americans. Washington offered George a position heading up the agricultural school at Tuskegee, and George accepted. Not only was it a way for George "to be of the greatest good to the greatest number of 'my people,'" it provided a welcome respite from the isolation of an all-white campus, where he was subjected to racial slurs and forced to eat in the kitchen of the dining hall.

George may have found more emotional support at Tuskegee, but he did not find adequate financial support. When he arrived, his modest budget forced him to stock the agricultural school's science laboratories with recycled materials like bottles, pots, wires, and tubes, which he rescued from trash bins. But, as he told his students, **"Ninety-nine percent of the failures come from people who have the habit of making excuses."** The extreme budget limitations he faced every day only better equipped him to serve the object of his research: the poor Southern farmer. He never forgot that "the primary idea in all of my work was to help the farmer and fill the poor man's empty dinner pail."

At the time of George's research, the greatest crisis facing black and white farmers alike was the legacy of sharecropping and an overdependence on the South's staple crops, cotton and tobacco. Farmers across the South were trapped in inefficient farming models, depleting the soil with uninterrupted years of nitrogen-leaching crops. George strove to find solutions that were accessible to small farmers and emphasized sweat equity and resource efficiency over fancy fertilizers and farm tools. But his greatest contribution was his championing of crop rotation, which led him to his most influential discovery: the peanut.

George was fascinated by the nitrogen-fixing bacteria that grow on the roots of the humble peanut and the sweet potato. He believed that by rotating these crops annually with high-demand cotton and tobacco, the average farmer could prevent soil depletion. His research showed that crop rotation worked, but he knew it would never catch on unless farmers were able to sell their peanut and sweet potato crops. And they would never be able to sell the crops unless George could find more uses for the often discarded tubers.

Over the next few decades, George Washington Carver became a household name as he enthusiastically developed and promoted 300 derivative products from peanuts, including peanut butter, shampoo, milk, cheese, mayonnaise, instant coffee, flour, soap, dyes, face powder, oil, adhesives, plastics, and pickles. His 118 products from sweet potatoes included vinegar, flour, starch, molasses, and even ink. He was called before a congressional committee to present his findings, and his research drew awards, including an honorary membership in the Royal Society for the Encouragement of Arts, Manufactures and Commerce in London. Yet he turned down a six-figured salaried position working with Thomas Edison to remain at Tuskegee. And out of all his inventions, he held only three patents, choosing to believe his ideas were the property of mankind: "God gave them to me. How can I sell them to someone else?"

At the time of George Washington Carver's death in 1943, peanuts had become a $200 million industry and the chief product of his home state, Alabama. For his contributions, George was honored with a Roosevelt medal for his role in restoring Southern agriculture. The little slave once known to neighbors as the "plant doctor" was now known around the world as the "Wizard of Tuskegee" and a savior to thousands of Southern farmers.

Carolyn McCarthy

When her husband and son became victims of gun violence, she took her fight for gun control all the way to Congress.

The Christmas tree was still in the yard. Which was odd, thought Carolyn McCarthy as she pulled her car into the driveway of her Long Island home on December 7, 1993, because she had asked her husband and son to bring it inside after they got home from work.

But also waiting in the yard was Carolyn's brother, who quickly broke the news: Carolyn's fifty-two-year-old husband, Dennis, and twenty-six-year-old son, Kevin, had been shot. On their way home from their jobs on Wall Street, a deranged man stood up on the Long Island Rail Road commuter train and began randomly firing at passengers. He emptied his clip of fifteen bullets, reloaded, and got off another fifteen shots. After the smoke cleared, nineteen passengers lay wounded—one of whom was Kevin. Another six passengers were dead—one of whom was Dennis.

While the Long Island Rail Road Massacre ended there, it had begun far away, in California, where Colin Ferguson purchased a gun and transported it illegally to New York. He had made sure to load it with Black Stallion bullets, an entirely legal design constructed to flare out upon impact to inflict maximum damage upon its victims.

As a nurse, Carolyn knew the weapon's capabilities, but nothing could prepare her for the extent of the bullets' power. When she arrived at the hospital, she found Kevin had been critically wounded and was given only a 10 percent chance of survival. He had sustained a hit to the head that blew away one-seventh of his brain, and his doctors gave him little chance of ever walking or talking again.

Months later, Carolyn reflected: "You learn from the disappointments and events that have been traumatic. . . . At the time, you think this is the worst thing that can happen to you. But **somehow you find the strength to get through it, and you go on."** Carolyn went on by seizing opportunities to speak out for stronger gun control measures. She traveled to Washington to rally support for the 1994 Crime Bill, which included a federal ban on nineteen assault weapons and the same fifteen-round clips that had killed her husband. The bill passed, but Carolyn was shocked to discover that her own district's congressman, Daniel Frisa, had voted against the ban. She confronted Frisa with her concerns and was ignored.

Never one to back down quietly, Carolyn responded with characteristic spunk when asked by a reporter if she was mad enough to run for Frisa's seat. "Sure," she replied, "I'm Irish—if I'm mad enough, I'll do it." The next day, the local papers announced Carolyn's candidacy.

Carolyn took the challenge head-on. She abandoned her lifelong allegiance to the Republican Party to take advantage of the Democratic Party's stronger stance on gun control. Afraid of being labeled a one-issue candidate, she strove to educate herself on all the relevant issues facing her constituents: health, education, foreign and domestic policy. With no experience in public service, the onus was on her to catch up with better-qualified candidates, both in her preparation for the job and in her campaigning skills.

Her challenges were as personal as they were political. Always a shy person, Carolyn found a camera and microphone in front of her at every turn. She had struggled with dyslexia her entire life and now found the prospect of poring over volumes of policy papers daunting.

She prepared most of all for a televised debate with Frisa, something she had initiated as a direct challenge to the incumbent congressman. When the night finally arrived, Frisa didn't. His decision to sit out the debate swung support overwhelmingly in her favor, and the election went to Carolyn McCarthy.

Since her election, Carolyn has been a driving force behind every major effort to decrease gun violence in this country, from raising awareness of child safety locks to collecting more accurate data on violence in our schools. She has worked tirelessly to close existing loopholes in firearm procurement and to fund better enforcement of current gun laws.

Carolyn's influence now extends beyond gun control. Once known as a single-issue candidate, today Carolyn McCarthy has transformed herself into an informed, opinioned political leader. *Newsday*, Long Island's newspaper, has consistently praised the local congresswoman for her "fair, open-minded" approach that "elevate[s] purpose above partisanship" and admired how "she has parlayed experience as a nurse and mother into a growing expertise and influence on health and education issues." Her honesty and integrity have garnered notice from all corners—from *Congressional Quarterly*, as one of the "CQ50" (50 most effective legislators in Congress) to *Ladies' Home Journal,* as one of the "100 Most Important Women of the 20th Century."

Throughout all of her political triumphs, Carolyn has also taken on the care and rehabilitation of her son. Today Kevin McCarthy not only walks and talks, but has returned to his job on Wall Street. He is a living symbol of Carolyn McCarthy's vow on the eve of that fateful shooting: "I promised my son, Kevin, that I would do everything I could . . . to make sure that what happened to our family doesn't happen to another one."

Martin Luther King, Jr.

The civil rights leader transformed one of the movement's greatest setbacks into a dry run for its most successful protest.

By 1963, Martin Luther King, Jr.'s, nonviolent protests–launched with the 1955 Montgomery, Alabama, bus boycott—were beginning to lose steam. While protests had been led by different groups around the South and Martin had become a nationally known figure, real progress was slow in coming.

Martin was active in leading the group he'd founded, the Southern Christian Leadership Conference (SCLC), trying to raise money and organize protests. But in 1961, he was asked to join a protest that had already started in Albany, Georgia. While Martin did not know much about the local group's strategy, he certainly supported their goals: desegregation of local restaurants, public restrooms, and other facilities. Martin lent his presence and name to the demonstrations, where there seemed to be a groundswell of support among black residents—at first.

But the demonstration ended futilely. The Albany movement was splintered by factions and backbiting, and many of the local leaders were resentful of Martin's last-minute appearance. There seemed to be no overall master plan for the protest. As hundreds of demonstrators were thrown in jail, no money was available to bail them out and no one had been recruited to fill their ranks on the street. Protesters became disillusioned, and the peaceful demonstrations soon dissolved into rioting, with local whites proclaiming proudly, "Albany is as segregated as ever." Most important, the protests garnered little media attention.

Martin was bitterly disappointed with the result and its implications for the movement in general. He contemplated stepping down from SCLC's leadership, tempted by a $100,000-a-year speaking engagement. But he turned down the offer on faith, hoping he could find a way to propel the movement forward.

Not long after, he heard about a burgeoning protest movement in Birmingham, Alabama, a place he called "the most thoroughly segregated city in the country." A local minister, Fred Shuttlesworth, was organizing a series of boycotts, sit-ins, and marches on the downtown merchants who segregated everything from department stores and restaurants to restrooms. Their police chief, Eugene "Bull" Connor, was known for his violent temper, outsized ego, and racist views. And Connor could expect nothing but support in a state where George Wallace had just been elected governor, announcing on the Capitol steps: "Segregation today. Segregation tomorrow. Segregation forever."

But the potential was great. If the protesters could loosen segregation's stranglehold on Birmingham, they could probably free the entire South. This time, Martin had learned from his mistakes in Albany. He knew an initial outpouring of righteous fervor would not be enough to sustain the Birmingham movement. As he prepared to march and almost certainly get arrested, he called on wealthy Northern SCLC supporters like Harry Belafonte to raise funds for the marchers' bail money. He ensured that the demonstrations were focused—in this case, on strictly economic targets. And he knew Bull Connor, with all of his hatred and venom, would prove to be the group's greatest ally, ensuring them a violent response that would attract the media attention they needed.

When he arrived in Birmingham, Martin found the same general skepticism and apathy that he'd left in Albany. But now, he spent more time in the churches, speaking for the cause and drumming up support. Among the organizers, he initially found the same factional infighting, but this time he made sure to work closely with the local groups to form a strong coalition. When he was inevitably arrested, he used the time to pen a response to local white clergymen and their full-page ad condemning the protests. This "Letter from a Birmingham Jail" was not just his personal manifesto, but the voice of the entire civil rights movement.

Despite all of his efforts, the movement sputtered out in the eight days Martin was in jail. It was Albany all over again. Hundreds of protesters still languished in jail, and no one volunteered to take their places on the streets. Faced with defeat, Martin was talked into a radical idea from one of his younger SCLC members. Since some of the most committed marchers were college students, why not recruit their younger siblings? Martin initially balked at the idea of putting high school and even grade school-aged children on the front lines, but reasoned that, with segregation, they walked the front lines every day.

So it was that on a warm spring day in 1963, 1,000 young people—some as young as six years old—marched to downtown Birmingham, singing and shouting for freedom. Bull Connor's men loaded 900 of them on buses and carted them off to juvenile court. But the next day, 2,500 children took to the streets, waving signs reading "Freedom." This time, Connor chose to try dispersing rather than arresting the demonstrators, but the peaceful scene quickly turned into turmoil. Firemen turned high-powered hoses on the children. Policemen clubbed them and chased them with German shepherds. As children fled the scene, Connor was heard to jeer, "Look at those niggers run."

It was a crushing defeat—but for the segregationists, not for the civil rights movement. Anticipating Connor's wrath, reporters from around the country had flocked to Birmingham and captured the brutal treatment for themselves. The front page of every major newspaper carried pictures of the attacks the next day. Film ran on the national news. And the tide of public opinion finally turned. The images galvanized blacks and moved moderate whites, including President John F. Kennedy and Attorney General Robert F. Kennedy, who had previously been too cautious to lend their full support to the movement.

With public opinion on his side, Martin intensified the demonstrations. Three thousand young people and adults marched on May 5, singing "I Want Jesus to Walk with Me." When the marchers stopped and knelt in prayer, Connor demanded, "Turn on the hoses." But this time, the firemen refused, some even breaking into tears. They fell away from the protest, overwhelmed by the power of nonviolence. The marchers had won the ultimate victory: they had won their enemies' hearts.

A few days later, downtown merchants agreed to come to the bargaining table. By the end of the week, every movement demand was met. Every lunch counter, restroom, fitting room, and drinking fountain in downtown Birmingham was now integrated.

But the movement didn't stop there. Inspired by the Birmingham example, other cities led demonstrations, and one by one, each city left segregation in its past. Martin's "Letter from a Birmingham Jail" became the defining statement of the movement, winning over thousands of people to civil rights causes. With the movement's momentum renewed, Martin helped plan the March on Washington. Within a year, his work was internationally acknowledged with the Nobel Peace Prize.

But Birmingham's greatest legacy was the establishment of nonviolent resistance as a legitimate and effective political tool. Through this movement's noble goals, it cleared the way for the Civil Rights Act of 1964, a gateway piece of legislation that ultimately resulted in protected rights for minorities, women, and people with disabilities. Through his commitment to nonviolence, Martin Luther King, Jr., showed the world that the ultimate setbacks—both injustice and the unjust persecution of its critics—could be used to transform the persecuted, the persecutors, and the world. When he wrote, **"I have attempted to see my personal ordeals as an opportunity to transcend myself,"** he asked the same of the entire nation.

Bernard Marcus

The founder of The Home Depot started the chain only after being fired from another hardware-store chain.

When Bernard "Bernie" Marcus moved to Atlanta to start a chain of discount hardware stores, he didn't have much to recommend him. He was fifty. He was broke. He was encumbered by a bitter lawsuit. And he had just been unceremoniously canned.

Humiliating failure wasn't something Bernie ever expected to be comfortable with. The son of a Russian-born cabinetmaker who didn't speak English, Bernie grew up in the roughest part of Newark, New Jersey. But like many immigrants, Bernie's parents had big dreams and high expectations for their son. "This is a golden country," his mother used to tell him. "You can be anything you want here." Above all, his parents taught him the lesson he would ultimately fall back on: believe in yourself.

Despite his inauspicious beginnings, Bernie eventually earned a degree in pharmacy from Rutgers University and went to work as a pharmacist in a friend's father's store. He soon realized he was far more interested in running the store than filling prescriptions. Since his friend's father didn't want a partner, Bernie left to help manage a discount store. His gift for salesmanship shined through, and he quickly moved up through a succession of highly successful discount, furnishings, and hardware stores.

By the late 1970s, Bernie was at a California chain of hardware stores called Handy Dan, where he had worked his way up to president and CEO. Unfortunately, he and his boss—the parent company's CEO—didn't get along. Sure, Bernie's confidence and frank outspokenness had gotten him in trouble before. But this time, Bernie found himself face-to-face with a control freak who resented not only Bernie's fierce independent streak but anyone else's. His boss second-guessed every decision and prided himself on his ruthlessness, calling himself "Ming the Merciless," after an old movie villain. He made sure Bernie knew that when an employee left his company, he would destroy them in every way possible—economically, professionally, and personally.

Still, Bernie wasn't too concerned. He was leading Handy Dan to unprecedented profits. The company had won the Home Center Retailer-of-the-Year Award, and was earning even more money than its parent company. And he was protected politically, because a close friend's investment group owned 19 percent of Handy Dan's stock—enough to block any moves Bernie didn't like.

But when the investment group sold out, Bernie was left vulnerable. And it didn't take too long for the inevitable to happen. Bernie and his right-hand man, Arthur Blank, were fired on a trumped-up labor violation dispute. The charge was later dismissed, but Bernard Marcus was still out of a job with no hefty severance package, no company stock to sell, no golden parachute. Just forty-nine and out of work.

His investor friend, however, was elated, telling Bernie, "You've just been hit in the ass by a golden horseshoe." He knew that Bernie had a vision of the ultimate home store, a store that would redefine the traditional hardware store and raise the industry's standard. Bernie's would be a megastore with the lower prices and wide variety of merchandise afforded by economies of scale, but with a knowledgeable and helpful staff of do-it-yourself experts unmatched by even the friendliest local hardware store. All Bernie needed was the money to start and an excuse to take the risk. The investor could get the money. And now Bernie finally had the excuse.

Bernie brought on Arthur Blank, and the two came across a chain called Homeco that was already putting many of their big ideas into practice. It was also teetering on the brink of bankruptcy. Rather than scrap their ideas, they convinced the owner, Pat Farrah, to join them in starting an entirely new venture: The Home Depot.

The ideas may have been big, but no one seemed to be very interested—at first. In the first year, the company lost $1 million out of its original $2 million investment. When they couldn't afford to fill the shelves with merchandise, they planted empty paint cans behind full ones and stacked empty boxes around the store to create the illusion of a full inventory.

Ultimately, people simply could not ignore the prices, which were aggressively advertised. And when they arrived in the store, they were amazed by the high quality of service. This is what Bernie had learned through the petty ugliness of his firing: be good to people, and they'll be good back to you.

Bernie became a disciple of what he called not customer service but customer cultivation. He trained sales associates so they would be able to answer any question a customer might have. He threatened to bite the finger off anyone who pointed to where a customer should go instead of walking over and showing them. He guaranteed that any customer would get any item they requested, even if it meant a Home Depot employee had to get in their car, drive to a competitor, pay the retail price, and hand-deliver it to the customer—which they did. When someone came into a store insisting on a refund on two tires, Bernie gave it to them, even though The Home Depot didn't sell tires. Bernie wanted to make sure every customer's experience at The Home Depot was a positive one, no matter what.

Of course, Bernie knew that the key to happy customers was happy employees. As his partner, Arthur Blank, later said: "When we left Handy Dan, we had made a ton of money for them but walked away with nothing. We vowed that if The Home Depot was successful, everyone who worked here would have a chance to share in the wealth." Bernie and Arthur instituted a values-based management system founded on respect for the customer and the employee. They awarded stock options to even the lowest-level employees and offered a no-risk stock-purchase plan for all employees at 15 percent below the market price (allowing them to get a refund on the difference if the stock price dropped). To dissuade sales associates from pushing unnecessary merchandise, they refused to pay commissions and instead paid 20 to 25 percent over competitors' salaries. They also created a foundation to support workers in times of need, providing funds to pay for new furniture for a family whose house burned down or a plane ticket for an employee to visit her dying mother.

Bernie also extended his own life lessons to his workforce, instilling in them what he took away from his greatest moment of defeat: **"You cannot be stopped by failure. Handling defeat is as important as handling success. . . .** The biggest problem of any single company in the world today is the inability to admit that you made a mistake. . . . We have taught our people that it's okay to make a mistake. You can make a mistake, as long as your heart was in the right place, as long as it was a judgment call, as long as there was honesty, that you did it because of good reasons. . . . It's okay to make a mistake."

Today, The Home Depot is the world's largest home-improvement retailer, with more than 1,500 stores. It has the highest net profit, the most sales per square foot, and the highest rate of return on equity in its industry. And as for this most impressive achievement, it was all born out of Bernie Marcus's greatest personal failure.

Steven Spielberg

Steven transformed every rejection he faced on his path to filmmaking into an alternative route to success.

It looked like a typical day in the life of Steven Spielberg. Dressed in a suit and carrying a briefcase, Steven walked past the guard at the Universal Studios lot, settled into his desk, took some phone calls, then wandered over to watch the day's filming. But on this day, he was not expected on the set, and his briefcase held nothing but his lunch. On this day, no one had heard of Steven Spielberg—a seventeen-year-old clerical intern working in Universal's purchasing division.

Steven, already an accomplished teenage filmmaker, had secured his position through Chuck Silvers, a friend of a friend of his father's who ran the Universal film library. Silvers had mentioned some clerical work that needed doing, but knew he couldn't get Steven a permanent pass to the lot. Steven dutifully showed up every day for the entire summer in his suit and his father's briefcase and casually slipped by the guard.

It was just what you'd expect from a kid who took his lifelong credo from the 1954 Disney movie, *Davy Crockett:* **"Be sure you're right and then go ahead."** And Steven's entire filmmaking career would indeed follow that advice. When Steven was only eight, his father received a Brownie 8 mm movie camera as a birthday gift. Steven quickly commandeered it, documenting every family vacation and even requiring his parents to restage events so he could capture them more "artistically." Impressed with his own ability to create a story, he next attempted to re-create his favorite action movie by filming a train wreck staged with his electric trains. The next year, he incorporated people into his storytelling technique (and earned his photography badge) by casting his Scout troop in a Western, *The Last Shoot-Out.*

By seventh grade, Steven's filmmaking talents were renowned throughout the neighborhood, and all the local kids got in on the act. Dressed in their fathers' old army uniforms, they traveled down to the airport, where Steven had gotten permission to shoot them in the cockpits of vintage fighter planes to make his World War II drama, *Fighter Squad.* He interspersed real documentary footage of midair dogfights among the overacted scenes of his ketchup-splattered friends pretending to be hit.

Soon adults began to sit up and take notice, too. Steven's film *Escape to Nowhere* won a statewide contest for struggling filmmakers, and the win was covered by the local news. *Firelight*—a precursor to *Close Encounters of the Third Kind*—which featured stop-motion animation and synced dialogue, music, and sound effects, was featured twice in the state newspaper and was treated to a Hollywood-like premiere at a downtown theater. By the time he completed *Firelight* at the age of seventeen, Steven was as knowledgeable and accomplished a filmmaker as many of those twice his age.

But this accomplishment came despite, or perhaps as a result of, a lifetime of personal pain. The oldest child of a computer engineer with IBM and a homemaker, Steven moved three times as he was growing up and endured all the difficulties that accompanied these disruptions. While his teachers recognized his intelligence, he put almost no effort into his studies, spending all his free time on his movies and receiving C's in return. He was an awkward, even geeky, child whose talent and skills were far better suited to filmmaking than to sports and popularity contests. Teased and sometimes bullied, Steven's unique interests set him apart from his classmates, as did his religious background. As the only Jew in increasingly Waspy suburbs, he was often greeted at school with ethnic slurs.

His home was no haven, either. His father worked long days, and Steven sorely missed his presence. But when his dad was home, the two fought bitterly about Steven's poor grades, especially in the sciences—a cardinal sin to Mr. Spielberg, who expected his son to become an engineer like himself. When not fighting with Steven, Mr. Spielberg fought with his wife, an artistic, nonconformist foil to his engineer mind-set. This rocky marriage eventually ended in divorce when Steven was in high school. Steven's lack of a supportive father figure would become a theme that appeared in many of his movies.

With both school and home as hostile territory, Steven escaped into the fantasy world of his movies. But while Steven told anyone who would listen about his plans to become "the Cecil B. DeMille of science fiction," his less-than-outstanding school record did not get him any closer to his goal. He applied to the state's two best film schools his senior year: the University of Southern California and the University of California at Los Angeles. Even with almost ten years of filmmaking experience and the recommendation of his mentor at Universal, he was flatly rejected.

Unwilling to give up, Steven enrolled in California State College at Long Beach, chosen for the degree it offered in television and radio and its proximity to the Hollywood lots. But the college couldn't match his own experience. A teacher there remembered, "Steve knew more about cameras than anybody in the department. He could *teach* the department." After seeing a short by USC student George Lucas, Steven tried again to transfer to a stronger film program. His study habits had followed him to college, where he often ditched class to watch movies all day at the local art cinema. His mediocre grades again held him back, and one professor even told him, "You're probably going to Vietnam anyway," referring to the steady stream of college dropouts who'd been drafted.

Finding no inspiration in a college education, Steven created his own education. He dusted off his jacket and briefcase and renewed his visits to the Universal lot. He hung around every department he could get into—filming, editing, sound mixing. He introduced himself to actors, directors, and producers and invited them to lunch. He sneaked onto movie sets and hung around until he was noticed and thrown off. Then he'd sneak back in. Steven later estimated he was thrown off a set a day.

When Steven tried to convince the Universal executives to watch one of his 8 mm student films, they told him they would consider only 16 mm. So Steven got a job at the college cafeteria, spent the money on film, rented a camera, and shot a new film in one weekend. When his mentor, Chuck Silvers, told him not to come back until he'd shot 35 mm, he did the same thing again, reappearing a few months later with what Silvers remembered as "what I still feel is the perfect motion picture."

That film was called *Amblin'*. A silent short about two drifters' existential crisis, it was a far cry from the sci-fi and wartime action movies Steven was used to directing. But it was an impressive piece of work—impressive enough to be circulated throughout the executive floor and to win the twenty-one-year-old Steven a seven-year contract with Universal. And after a few stints directing TV dramas and low-budget features, Steven was given his first break directing a big Hollywood movie: a thriller starring a shark.

Jaws broke box office records and put Steven Spielberg on the map, forging a relationship with Universal that would produce *E.T.*, *Jurassic Park*, and *Schindler's List*. As his first producer reflected, "It's not an accident Spielberg is where he is." Steven's all-consuming passion for filmmaking elevated him above rejection, prejudice, and skepticism and gave him the unshakable faith in his own abilities that allowed him to forge ahead.

It also gave him the last laugh. Once rejected from USC, Steven Spielberg today holds an honorary doctorate from the school and sits on the board of trustees.

Wilma Rudolph

Once told she would never walk, she would go on to run her way to three Olympic gold medals.

By the time Wilma Rudolph was four years old, she had already attained perhaps her life's greatest achievement: survival. Born two months premature, she weighed only 4.5 pounds. Since the only hospital to accept black patients was an hour away, her mother chose to nurse her to health at home. Her mother would see her through an alarming succession of childhood illnesses: measles, mumps, chicken pox, and then scarlet fever and double pneumonia at the same time. When Wilma's left leg gradually began to weaken and deform, her mother did whatever she could to alleviate the child's discomfort. But as the leg worsened, Wilma's mother boarded a Greyhound bus and took Wilma and what little money they had to the hospital in Nashville.

It was polio, the doctor said—a disease that terrified any parent in the 1940s. At the time, there was no cure, and the disease could spread and paralyze the lungs or nervous system. Fortunately for

Wilma, the disease seemed to be confined to her leg. Unfortunately, said the doctor, she would never be able to walk.

Wilma's mother had other ideas, and the two began a weekly ritual. Twice a week, they would board the back of that Greyhound bus and travel the hour each way to Nashville. Wilma would perform hours of painful physical therapy exercises designed to strengthen her leg. Not walking was never an option to Wilma or her mother. "The doctors told me I would never walk, but my mother told me I would," she later wrote, "so I believed in my mother." By the time Wilma was six, she was given metal leg braces to help her walk.

She spent most of her time trying to get out of them. She likened them to convicts' chains, for even though they allowed her to walk, they forced her to stay home from school. As the twentieth of twenty-two children, Wilma had plenty of opportunity to see kids leaving for school, running around the yard, and talking about their classes and schoolmates. Feeling left behind, she sank into a deep depression, crying at home alone.

And then one day, she got mad. It seemed completely unfair, to that girl of six, that she should be sitting on the sidelines of life while everyone else got to participate. She later wrote in her autobiography, "So I started getting angry about things, fighting back in a new way, with a vengeance. I think I started acquiring a competitive spirit right then and there, a spirit that would make me successful in sports later on. I was mad, and I was going to beat these illnesses no matter what."

She continued her physical therapy at home, her brothers and sisters helping her complete the exercises and massaging her legs. The next year, she went to school with the leg braces on, and a few years later, she caused an uproar at church when she walked bravely down the aisle one Sunday—no braces, just Wilma on her own two feet.

By the time she entered junior high, she was ready to join the basketball team. Against her mother's wishes, she begged the coach to let her play. He relented, but benched Wilma for three years, letting her play only in the last few seconds of losing games and sometimes not even letting her suit up. It was three long years of frustration for Wilma, and three long years of preparation, too. Wilma's years of watching other children play while she sat on the sidelines had taught her the powers of observation. She watched. She studied. She analyzed. She arrived on the court with a keen understanding of the game that rivaled her coach's.

After three years of waiting, Wilma demanded her coach put her in the game. He put her in the starting lineup, where she led her team to an undefeated season and the state championships. The team lost the championship title, but Wilma won something much greater: the attention of the women's track coach at Tennessee State University. The "Tigerbelles" were the premiere women's track team in the region, and Coach Temple invited Wilma to join the team, even though she was still in high school.

Wilma had run a little track at school, although the meets were informal races where no one thought to record times or placements. She always won easily in her meets: "Running, at the time, was nothing but pure enjoyment for me. I was winning without really working." Wilma was in for a rude awakening under Coach Temple. He was strict, requiring the girls to run an extra lap for every minute they were late to practice. One morning, Wilma overslept by a half hour. Thirty laps later, she resolved to be a half hour early to practice from then on.

The training wasn't the biggest shock. At her first official track meet, Wilma lost every race she ran. She found herself passed time and again by athletes with better training and technique. Though defeated, she was determined to improve her own skills. She worked with Coach Temple to learn breathing technique and race strategy. She practiced her starts, always her weak link. She built up physical strength and mental stamina. She also began to see the older college athletes as fellow competitors, not heroes. She stopped holding back and gave herself permission to beat these more seasoned athletes.

The training worked. Wilma had never even heard of the Olympics until the Tigerbelles invited her to join them for the 1956 tryouts. But she made the team and—this girl from rural Tennessee who had never left the South—traveled to Australia to participate in the Melbourne Olympics. At the tender age of sixteen, Wilma won a bronze in the 4 x 100-meter relay and was thrilled to stand on the platform with her teammates, all Tigerbelles. But Wilma didn't even make the finals in her own races. Watching her opponents accepting their medals, she vowed to return in 1960.

Wilma spent the next four years in intensive training, winning a full scholarship to Tennessee State to officially join the Tigerbelles. In 1960, she made the Olympic Team again and traveled to Rome to compete in three separate events. While runners from other countries struggled in the 100-degree heat, Wilma found it just like another humid summer in Tennessee. Despite a sprained ankle, this time she easily won her heats and—more surprisingly—her finals, breaking the world record in the 100-meter dash (although thrown out because of a strong tailwind) and the Olympic record in the 200-meter dash. After easy gold medals in the 100- and 200-meter events, she joined her Tigerbelles in the 400-meter relay, setting again a world record in the first heat. In the finals, the team was set for another clean win until Wilma almost dropped the baton, giving Germany and Russia the lead. Refusing to cost her team the medal, she burst ahead, passing her opponents and crossing the finish line only three-tenths of a second ahead.

Wilma had become the first American woman to win three gold medals in the Olympics, earning the title "the Fastest Woman in the World." She was invited across Europe and around the world for exhibition races. The European press fell in love with her, calling her the "Black Gazelle." But Wilma's greatest tribute was the Clarksville, Tennessee, homecoming parade in her honor. Remembering her days on the back of the Greyhound bus, Wilma insisted that the town throw out their segregation laws for all her homecoming events. The town fathers complied, and her parade and banquet were the first integrated events the town had ever seen.

Wilma went on to stay active in her sport—coaching high school, bringing sports to inner-city youth, covering track on television, even starting her own foundation for amateur athletes. She mentored African-American female Olympic athletes like Jackie Joyner-Kersee and Florence Griffith Joyner, the next woman to win three Olympic gold medals. These women and the thousands of other athletes Wilma counseled were inspired by her spirit and her ultimate life lesson: **"The triumph can't be had without the struggle."**

Walt Disney

Before there was Mickey, there was Alice, Oswald the Rabbit—and bankruptcy.

Walt Disney was born in Chicago in 1901, but he was not destined to stay there long. Walt and his four siblings spent their childhood following their father from one failed business opportunity to another, moving from Florida, to Chicago, to a farm in Missouri, to Kansas City, and back to Chicago again.

Walt's father had been hardened by a lifetime of petty successes and pestering failures and was known for being critical and sometimes violent. He expected his sons to invest sweat equity in whatever fruitless endeavor he was currently pursuing. Nine-year-old Walt was first recruited on his father's extensive paper route. He later recounted waking up at 3:30 A.M. on cold winter mornings and stopping to play with toys the children on his route had forgotten in their yards.

His father's one indulgence was the most life-changing. Walt took drawing classes every Saturday at the Kansas City Art Institute and School of Design, which his father deemed "educational." Walt was quick to turn his talent into a moneymaking venture. Toward the end of World War I, Walt dropped out of high school to join the corps of ambulance drivers and found surprising success drawing pictures and caricatures for U.S. soldiers. Buoyed by this vote of confidence, he returned home after the war with the idea of joining the *Kansas City Star* as an apprentice to the staff cartoonist. With little education and no family connections, he was turned down for the job.

Walt used his wartime sketches instead to secure a job with an outfit called the Kansas City Film Ad Company, which produced short animated advertisements shown in local movie theaters. With the techniques he learned on the job, the enterprising Walt soon started his own company called Laugh-O-Gram, using his own drawings to make spoof newsreels, animated fairy tales, and even a dental hygiene film. Optimistic about the industry's future, he raised $15,000 from investors and sold a series of cartoons to a Kansas City theater.

While Walt's staff set to work on the series, the company struggled to keep afloat. Walt gave up his apartment and slept in his office and relied on kindly neighboring restaurant owners for free meals. When his lone client filed bankruptcy six months later with only one film in the series finished, Walt followed suit.

Walt later said, "It's important to have a good, hard failure when you're young." And true to his word, he would have more. He left Kansas City with only $40—the proceeds from the sale of his Laugh-O-Gram movie camera—and joined his brother Roy in California with the hope of reviving the Laugh-O-Gram series in Hollywood. He resurrected the newsreel spoof briefly for a Los Angeles movie theater and sold a film-series idea—a take on *Alice in Wonderland* that juxtaposed a live-action little girl against a cartoon background—to a film distributor in New York named Charles Mintz. At $1,500 a film, this was Walt's big break.

Walt and Roy set up business together; they sent back to Kansas City for one of Walt's old friends to do the illustrations and gradually built up a staff of apprentices. After their contract was renewed twice, Mintz and his brother-in-law, George Winkler, felt the Alice concept was worn out and asked to see something new.

Walt came up with a series about a mischievous rabbit named Oswald, the first of many cuddly and comic animals to come. The series took off, surpassing the Alice series immediately. By now, the Disneys had arrived. At $2,250 a reel, both brothers had finally gotten married, bought their first houses in a respectable area, and renovated a storefront into a legitimate working studio.

With the arrangement with Mintz going so smoothly, the brothers were surprised that his partner, Winkler, insisted on traveling all the way out to California each month to deliver their check and pick up the new installment. The next time Walt was in New York, he uncovered the underlying reason for Winkler's visits out West. Walt traveled to Mintz's office to propose a raise in rates, only to find his proposal met with a demand to cut his fees and join Mintz's own operation. If he didn't, Walt would lose his entire staff, whom Winkler had been discreetly cajoling during his visits behind the scenes with promises of pay raises and greater artistic freedom. What was worse, whether Walt signed on or not, he would lose his most important equity: the rights to Oswald the Rabbit, which Mintz had made sure to license under his own name.

An older and wiser Walt later mused, **"You may not realize it when it happens, but a kick in the teeth may be the best thing in the world for you."** But this young and naive Walt walked out, losing his staff and his work in the space of one meeting. Both his business and his artistic creations had been wiped out, leaving him right where he was when he arrived in Hollywood with little more than pocket change and an idea. While he had the capital now, what he needed desperately was another great idea—something better than Oswald the Rabbit, something that could put him on the map again.

Like most legendary ideas, this idea's origins are still contested. Walt himself suggested that the sound of the train on his way back to California whispered, *"Chug, chug, mouse, chug, chug, mouse."* Other accounts tell of a mouse he kept in his Kansas City studio, feeding and training it and ultimately releasing it in "the best neighborhood I could find" when he left for California.

Whatever the mouse's origins, it was soon dressed in red velvet pants with big white buttons and christened Mortimer. Mrs. Disney reportedly found that name too pretentious and suggested a name more fitting to Walt's humble Midwestern roots: Mickey.

When Walt got back to the studio, he frantically set about producing a new movie with a "Mickey" prototype designed for ease of drawing, using circles for ears "so they could be drawn the same, no matter how he turned his head" and simplified hands with only four fingers. After the premiere of *The Jazz Singer,* Hollywood's first movie with sound, Walt saw his opportunity to capitalize on the phenomenon and quickly got to work on a new feature, *Steamboat Willie.* Using a metronome to pace out the reel, he filled the audio track with slide whistles, pots and pans, cowbells, and New Year's noisemakers, and his own voice for Mickey.

The first "talkie" cartoon was just the sensation Walt knew it would be. It was bought by the manager of the Colony Theater in New York, who treated the film as a "special attraction," drumming up press coverage. Once the run began on September 19, 1928, distributors were coming to Walt, begging to buy *Steamboat Willie* and future Disney films to show around the country. Walt built his studio back up based on the sale of the Mickey series and started churning out more adventures of Mickey—not to mention Donald, Daisy, Pluto, Goofy, and the rest of the Disney menagerie.

But Walt was still smarting from the Oswald the Rabbit incident and consequently made a key business decision when he sold his first Mickey series: he insisted on keeping artistic control over his work and maintaining rights to his characters. It had been a painful lesson but ultimately perhaps his most important one, for it secured his control over the Disney enterprise. Today, that legacy encompasses not just cartoons but a media empire beyond Walt's wildest dreams.

Nelson Mandela

Twenty-seven years of brutal treatment in prison only strengthened South Africa's future president's perseverance and political influence.

"I was not born with a hunger to be free. I was born free," Nelson Mandela wrote in his autobiography. Growing up on the open plains of the Transkei region in South Africa, Nelson enjoyed a relatively privileged position as the son of an important counselor to the tribal chief. He spent his days playing with the other village children and herding the family's livestock. He would also spend hours watching his father counsel the chief, and he absorbed how the chief listened patiently to every petition and opinion offered, shaping a decision that would be fair to everyone. Nelson, whose birth name, "Rohihlahla," can be translated as "troublemaker," had no idea how important this lesson would be.

Nelson's pastoral childhood came to an abrupt halt with the death of his father. He was sent to live with the local governor, a friend of his father's, who took charge of the boy's education and enrolled him at the best schools available to black youth. Nelson distinguished himself as a student, but when his guardian tried to force him into an arranged marriage, he ran away to Johannesburg, where he secured work at a law firm. After earning a law degree, he opened his own firm.

Although Nelson's career and family were becoming established, Johannesburg brought his very freedom into question. Lives of white and black citizens were in stark contrast there, with luxury and stability on one side and overwhelming poverty pervading the shanty-filled townships on the other. Nelson was shocked at the limitations placed on his prospects and the daily indignities he suffered under the policy of apartheid, or "separation," much like the segregation of the American South. He joined his local chapter of the African National Congress (ANC), a political party committed to equal rights for native Africans and a democratic society for all, and quickly moved into a position of leadership.

Under the oppressive apartheid government's regime, Nelson and his fellow ANC supporters were soon brought to court on treason charges. Even after they were acquitted of all charges, the protesters were subject to constant harassment and surveillance by the government's police forces. Nelson went underground, disguising himself from the police so successfully that he became known as "the Black Pimpernel."

Nelson escaped notice long enough to leave the country to raise funds for the ANC from other African nations. However, upon reentering South Africa, he was seized by the police and brought up on charges of illegal emigration, soon followed by far more serious charges of sabotage. This time, the court was not lenient. He and the rest of the ANC leadership received life sentences.

Life in prison meant life in one of South Africa's most notorious facilities: Robben Island. The ANC prisoners received a "D" classification, that of the prison's most dangerous inmates with the fewest privileges. They were each given a cell with a straw mat and a thin blanket for a bed and an iron bucket for a toilet. All three meals were the same: a meager corn porridge with perhaps a vegetable or a gristly piece of meat thrown in at dinnertime. The men wore thin khaki shirts and shorts, even in the wintertime, and were denied access to any newspapers and magazines—in fact, to any news at all. The prisoners spent most hours of their day in the lime quarry, where they toiled under exhausting physical labor.

As one of the group's leaders, Nelson received harsher treatment than others. He underwent periods of solitary confinement: twenty-three hours a day alone in a cell where a single bulb burned all day and all night, making it impossible to sleep or to tell what time it was. He was allowed only one visitor every six months and once went two years without seeing his wife, Winnie. He could write and receive only one letter every six months. The letters he did receive were censored by his guards, who would cut out offending sections with a razor, effectively deleting in the process even more writing on the back.

Still, "Any man or institution that tries to rob me of my dignity will lose," Nelson wrote in a letter smuggled out of prison. He and his fellow inmates conspired to subvert their captors' authority however possible and developed ways to pass notes between prisoners and even prisoners' blocks. At first, Nelson would replace the bottom of a used matchbox with paper containing virtually microscopic writing, then drop the matchbox in the exercise yard for another prisoner to pick up. When rain scuttled these plans, they began wrapping notes in plastic and leaving them in food bins or taping them inside shared toilet bowls. For extra security, they wrote messages with milk, which when dried became invisible until sprayed with the disinfectant they used to clean their cells. Nelson used a favorite method—filling a square of toilet paper with tiny writing to be smuggled out to visitors—to write his autobiography while still in prison, even though newspapers and publishing houses throughout South Africa were forbidden to write about or photograph him.

The ANC prisoners found their greatest strength in knowledge, a source of power they strove to share with as many prisoners as possible. They quickly got permission to study and pursue degrees by correspondence, and so many prisoners received advanced degrees that the prison came to be known as "the University." The name also reflected the system of study groups the ANC established within the prison. Divided into work groups in the quarry, the prisoners transformed these sessions into lectures and study halls, led by senior ANC members who spoke at length on a number of academic subjects. At any given time, the inmates were immersed in English, Afrikaans, art, geography, and mathematics. They received additional instruction from their fellow captives in political history and philosophy. Nelson even acted in a performance of *Antigone*. Despite the guards' efforts to crush the ANC infrastructure, the close proximity of the prisoners allowed them to train new members, thus consolidating and strengthening the organization from the inside.

Education didn't end with the prisoners. As Nelson later wrote, "It was ANC policy to try to educate all people, even our enemies: we believed that all men, even prison service warders [guards], were capable of change, and we did our utmost to try to sway them."

The longer Mandela remained in prison, the louder the demands grew for his freedom and the more galvanized the movement became. The government tried twice to barter with him for his release, once by asking Nelson to accept exile in the Transkei and once by insisting he ask his followers to renounce violence as a means to win the struggle. On both counts, he refused and demanded his own release, claiming, "A prisoner cannot enter into contracts. Only a free man can."

As violence swelled between police and demonstrators and international sanctions against apartheid threatened the country's economy, the government agreed to engage in true negotiations with Mandela. Nelson met secretly with President Pieter Botha, then President Frederik de Klerk. He refused all offers of deals and compromises until he was given the ANC's chief demands: the immediate release of all political prisoners, a lift of all bans on political organizations, and the ending of the years-old nationwide state of emergency that had suspended many Africans' civil rights. A few days later, President de Klerk appeared in front of the nation and announced a plan to end the system of apartheid and replace it with a more inclusive democracy.

De Klerk immediately set into motion Mandela's release. On February 11, 1990, when Nelson walked out of prison, holding his wife's hand, he was greeted by thousands of people chanting, cheering, and waving flags and banners. He raised his fist and called out the traditional ANC rallying cry, *"Amandla!"* ("Power!"), to which they responded, *"Ngawethu!"* ("The power is ours!")

Mandela and de Klerk received the Nobel Peace Prize in 1993. By the next year, Nelson Mandela assumed the role he had spent thirty years preparing for: president of a newly democratic South Africa.

Nelson Mandela has been known to say, **"The struggle is my life,"** by which he refers to South Africa's struggle against a tyrannical government. But it is an equally valid interpretation that, for Mandela, the point of life is struggle: to overcome obstacles, to expect more of one's neighbors, to challenge oneself. For it is in the struggle that Nelson Mandela found his own—and his country's—greatness.

Betty Friedan

Betty's own stifled career ambitions led her to write the explosive book that helped launch the women's liberation movement.

In 1944, Betty Friedan was working as a reporter for the labor press, covering job discrimination against black and Jewish workers. With a child at home, she considered herself lucky to be one of the rare professional women at the time who both worked and had a family. But like many women of her generation, whatever promise she showed led to a not-so-promising future. When she became pregnant with her second child, she was fired and told, "It's your fault for being pregnant again." The labor movement's sympathy for job discrimination did not extend to pregnant women.

It was a bitter pill for Betty to swallow. She was more than qualified for the job, having graduated summa cum laude from Smith, where she had been a Phi Beta Kappa and editor of the student paper. Her academic record was so impressive that she won a scholarship to pursue graduate work at the University of California at Berkeley, and her first year of work there won her yet another award—a prestigious fellowship that would pay for her Ph.D. in psychology. However, she turned it down.

Opinions differ on the reasons behind this controversial decision. She later wrote that she found academic work too far removed from the radical activism that had caught her interest. Other sources cite her fear that becoming a teacher meant ending up a spinster, since teachers at the time were often fired when they got married. In *The Feminine Mystique*, Betty wrote that her then boyfriend's jealousy prompted her to bow out, as she was unwilling to seem more talented or ambitious than her mate. But she also admitted that, "I never could explain, hardly knew myself, why I gave up this career. . . . But for years afterward, I could not read a word of the science that once I had thought of as my future life's work; the reminder of its loss was too painful."

Though she was determined not to give up an opportunity again, with the loss of her reporting job, Betty was quickly relegated to full-time motherhood in the suburbs. She tried to stay occupied. She organized a program that brought local professionals into high schools to talk about career paths. She submitted articles to women's magazines, finding that she had to speak down to her audience to get published. She had another child. She felt increasingly trapped in a turbulent marriage. While she enjoyed motherhood, she did not feel it was enough to keep her intellectually stimulated. Overcome by feelings of futility, frustration, and guilt at not finding fulfillment with the role of wife and mother, she yearned to establish an identity outside her family.

For her fifteenth Smith reunion in 1957, Betty sent a questionnaire to all her classmates, asking them what they had achieved since they left college and how they felt about their prospects. She was overwhelmed by the response. Hundreds of women wrote that they shared Betty's feelings. They had a first-rate education but had never been encouraged to pursue a career. They loved their families but felt they were losing themselves. They struggled with depression, anxiety, malaise—the classic signs of an identity crisis. They had lost their sense of self because, as Betty famously wrote, **"it is easier to live through someone else than to become complete yourself."**

The reporter in Betty smelled a story in the making. She wrote up an article describing the phenomenon—what she called "the problem that has no name"—and submitted it to all the major women's magazines. The editors at McCall's rejected it, suggesting she was making it up. The editors at Ladies' Home Journal rewrote it every time she submitted it, to say the exact opposite of what she meant. Another editor accused her of being "sick" for admitting her dissatisfaction, and *Redbook* told her agent, "Betty has gone off her rocker. She has always done a good job for us, but this time only the most neurotic housewife could identify."

With no magazine willing to publish the article, Betty decided to try to turn it into a book instead. She worked on the book every day for five years while her children were at school, finding more and more evidence of this silent crisis among American women. When she finally finished the book, her own agent refused to represent the work. Forced to represent herself, she finally found a publisher willing to take her book, although they agreed to print only a few thousand copies.

Betty titled the book *The Feminine Mystique*, finally naming the societal forces that conspired to keep women out of the workforce and in the kitchen. It suggested that society used consumerism to create a cult of domesticity that encouraged Rosie the Riveter to drop her drill and buy a new vacuum cleaner. It promoted a vision in which women shared household and breadwinning duties with their husbands and reclaimed their selfhood. It not only captured the experience of women across the country but clarified Betty's own. "My whole life had prepared me to write that book," she confessed. "All the pieces of my own life came together for the first time in the writing of it." By 1966, the book had sold more than 3 million copies.

The book helped launch the women's liberation movement. Betty Friedan became a household name and she began lecturing at universities and city halls around the country. In 1966, she founded the National Organization for Women to help enforce the Civil Rights Act of 1964, the law that gave legal protection to women against discrimination. Today, Betty's response to the obstacles she faced has enabled women around the world to face *their* obstacles, creating successes and failures that are uniquely their own.

Spence Silver and Art Fry

A failed invention became one of the most popular new products of the century, thanks to a little persistence.

Like many great inventions, the innocuous and ubiquitous Post-it note was born out of a mistake. It later became not only the business world's preferred communication vehicle but 3M's ticket back to industry leadership and solvency.

As far back as 1968, 3M chemist Spence Silver was working on ways to improve the acrylate adhesives that gave many common household tapes their "stick." One day, he developed a polymer cement that defied any expectations he may have held.

It wouldn't stick. It wouldn't dry. It would create a bond between two surfaces but wouldn't hold to either. In short, it preferred to cling to its own molecules rather than to any other—not exactly what a chemist is looking for in a usable tape. What it would do was adhere lightly, creating a temporary bond—a use that Spence felt strongly must be good for something.

Unwilling to throw the findings out, Spence kept playing with and pushing the discovery for years. He created a spray-can application. He invented a bulletin board that was covered with the adhesive and could hold papers without pushpins. He finally began holding seminars for fellow 3M employees in the hope that one of them might have a better idea than his.

One of those seminar attendees was Art Fry, a fellow chemist and an avid member of his church choir. He was continually frustrated in his attempts to hold his place in his hymnal; scraps of paper slipped out, and heftier bookmarks made it hard to hold several places at once. But one Sunday morning, after another round of losing his place, he finally stumbled onto his solution during a dull sermon: "My mind was wandering back to the music problem when I had one of those 'flashes of insight.' Eureka! I think I could make a bookmark, using Dr. Silver's adhesive, that would stick and remove without damaging the book."

Art had finally unlocked the possibilities of the mystery adhesive, but when he and Spence teamed up to create the prototype, they were told the company didn't have the equipment necessary to coat pads of paper with it. Art was thrilled: "That is great news! **If it were easy, then anyone could do it.** If it really is as tough as you say, then 3M is the company that can do it." With characteristic tenacity, he developed his own equipment in his basement, building it so large that he ultimately had to knock out a basement wall to take the machine back to his lab at 3M.

Up to this point, Art and Spence still thought of their prototype as a bookmark. Its evolution began when Art posted one on a research report and scribbled a note on it for a colleague. The coworker lifted the note and reattached it to another report he was passing on to Art. Art later remembered, "It was during a coffee break that afternoon when we both realized that what we had was not just a bookmark but a new way to communicate or organize information." What they had was a Post-it note.

Not one to be undone by an obstacle like a basement wall, Art was hardly deterred by his next obstacle: the marketing department, who saw no sales potential in the invention. Art and Spence knew the product would sell itself if only people knew what to do with it. They made up hundreds of pads and distributed them to the company's senior executives. When supplies ran low, the now-hooked execs begged for more, and Art and Spence routed all their calls straight to the marketing department.

With marketing finally sold on the idea, there remained one last key audience to convince: 3M's customers. The first test markets in Richmond, Virginia, and Boise, Idaho, were a failure with consumers, who didn't see the point in paying extra for a small, colorful notepad. Still persistent, 3M sent sales reps door-to-door in Richmond and Boise to give the pads away to businesses, perform free demos in banks and stores, and addict everyone who used the sticky notes.

When the Post-it note was finally launched nationally in 1980, it became an integral part of office and home life. It also renewed 3M's fortunes by creating a not-too-sticky empire. As Spence suspected back in 1968, the polymer had multiple uses, which now include not only a variety of Post-it note sizes but also file-folder tabs, phone message pads, tape flags, glue sticks, and removable transparent tape.

Can failure result in success? 3M must think so. 3M scientists today are required to spend 15 percent of their working hours toying with new ideas—even if their ideas don't work and have no immediate marketable application.

Louis Armstrong

This jazz great's career was born in the slums of New Orleans and launched by a stay in juvenile hall.

According to his own legend, Louis Armstrong was born to a very poor New Orleans family on the Fourth of July, 1900. (His baptismal certificate reveals the true date to be August 4, 1901.) He was almost immediately abandoned by his father, and his mother, a teenager probably forced into prostitution to make ends meet, entrusted his care to her mother.

Though as poor as Louis's parents, his grandmother Josephine instilled a sense of dignity in the young boy. A washerwoman, she believed fiercely in the American work ethic and often remarked, "The only person who ever made his living sitting down was the shoemaker." By the time he returned to his mother's house at age five, he was used to getting a nickel every time he helped pick up and deliver his grandmother's washing.

Fortunately, like her own mother, Louis's mother, Mayann, was loving and strict, an oasis of calm in the chaos that was the New Orleans slums. Louis always credited her for his later success, remembering, "My mother had one thing . . . and that was **good common sense and respect for human beings, yea. That's my diploma."** But despite Mayann's best efforts, Louis spent most of his childhood in poverty, often shoeless and almost always hungry.

By the time Louis was seven, he was sent out into the streets to bring home money. He sang on street corners for spare change and rifled through garbage for semirotten produce to sell to disreputable restaurants. His most important job, however, was on a junk wagon owned by the Karnoffskys, a family of Russian immigrants. The Karnoffskys treated Louis like a member of the family, feeding him dinner and teaching him Russian lullabyes. Louis was impressed by their commitment to work and their drive to climb their way out of poverty.

Louis loved his job, both for the camaraderie and the chance to see the city that lay outside his squalid neighborhood. In his daily travels, he was exposed to the variety of music only New Orleans is known for: brass bands playing in funeral parades, ragtime and blues drifting out of seedy honky-tonks, church hymns from Catholic masses and Baptist revivals alike. Louis best loved delivering buckets of coal to the prostitutes in Storyville, where he could linger to hear his hero, King Oliver, playing the cornet at a neighborhood dive.

His love of music didn't go unnoticed, so when Louis found a discarded tin horn on the junk wagon and started blowing it to attract business, the Karnoffskys loaned him the money to buy a real cornet. Louis taught himself to play the instrument by picking out popular tunes: "I realized I could play 'Home Sweet Home'—then here come the blues." Pretty soon, kids were bringing old bottles to the wagon just to hear Louis play. The Karnoffskys loved it, and so did passersby. Louis couldn't help but notice that his playing brought joy to everyone who heard it: rich or poor, black or white. It was a discovery that would become the foundation of his musical philosophy.

As Louis became more adventurous on his horn, he became more rebellious on the streets. He stole newspapers from white newsboys (the only ones allowed to sell them) and jumped on moving streetcars to resell them. He wasn't beyond hustling fifty cents off a gullible adult. The school he had sporadically attended was finally left behind.

An adolescent prank would finally rip Louis away from his squalid but nurturing environment. On New Year's Eve when he was thirteen, he joined in the festivities by firing his stepfather's pistol in the air. He was promptly arrested by a nearby policeman and sentenced to the Colored Waif's Home for Boys, where he lived for the next year and a half. The home was strict, even spartan: the boys were drilled in military exercises and fed beans, brown bread, and molasses.

However, the home did have a renowned marching band. And Louis, his cornet left behind, ached to join. He begged the band director, Peter Davis, for a chance to audition. But Mr. Davis was leery of young Louis, whom he branded a troublemaker. For six months, he put off Louis's requests, but he finally relented and invited the boy to band practice. When Louis arrived, he was handed . . . a tambourine. It was weeks before Mr. Davis let him graduate to an alto horn. Then a bugle. And finally the cornet.

Under Mr. Davis's watchful eye, Louis practiced his horn every chance he got. He undertook to remodel the mouthpiece by hand for a better range of sound. Mr. Davis took Louis to his own home on weekends to let him practice hymns with his daughter on the piano. Storyville may have given Louis his first musical training, but Mr. Davis gave him life training: discipline, moral judgment, and a firm belief in himself. After a year under the band director's tutelage, Louis was given the highest (and probably only) honor of his short life: he was appointed leader of the Waif's Home band.

It was a job Louis took seriously, especially on the day when the band took part in a parade that would be routed through his old neighborhood. All the gamblers and pimps and hustlers came out for the event and were delighted to see little "Dippermouth" leading the band, playing his heart out on his beat-up cornet. They threw money his way— big bills now, not just the pennies he had sung for in his youth—and Louis collected so much cash, he was able to buy new uniforms and instruments for the entire band.

Louis Armstrong had arrived, displaying the characteristic talent, leadership, and generosity that would distinguish him throughout his career. By the time he was twenty-one, he would leave New Orleans to follow his mentor, King Oliver, to Chicago. By the time he was thirty-five, he would tour through Europe with his own band and appear on Broadway, in film, and on the radio. By the time he died, he would be known worldwide as the granddaddy of jazz and as an undisputed musical genius.

But Louis's real path to greatness began with that ill-conceived prank. "That shot, I do believe," he later reminisced, "started my career. My whole success goes back to the time I was arrested as a wayward boy of thirteen. Because then I *had* to quit running around and began to learn something. Most of all, I began to learn music."

Suze Orman

Life taught her the tough financial lessons that she passed on to her readers.

When Suze Orman was thirteen, she saw her father run into a burning building—the take-out shack he owned on Chicago's South Side. Moments later, he staggered out clutching the white-hot metal cash register containing the day's receipts. As he dropped the register, the skin from his arms and chest fell with it.

Money, this working-class daughter of Russian immigrants realized, mattered.

But it didn't matter right away for Suze. A lifelong speech impediment and reading disability drove her to drop out of college and join friends on a cross-country trip to California. She picked up shifts at a bakery in Berkeley, where she waited tables for the next seven years at $400 a week.

Despite Suze's meager beginnings, she had a bigger dream. She envisioned a hot-tub-and-sauna spa with an on-site restaurant and hair salon, right there in Berkeley. Her customers at the bakery heard bits and pieces of her plan, until one day one of her regulars handed her a check for $2,000. It was a loan, he said, at zero percent interest, to be paid back in ten years. Slowly other customers chipped in, and before long, she had amassed $50,000 in start-up funds.

Knowing nothing about investing herself, Suze took the money to a respected brokerage and asked for a safe, stable investment. Instead, the broker put her in oil options, one of the riskiest, most volatile stock ventures. While Suze didn't complain when she saw 10 percent returns in the first few weeks, she was shocked when the market quickly reversed and her money disappeared.

Fortunately, the brokerage took responsibility for their employee's ineptitude, paying back Suze's losses. She took the money, promptly paid off her investors, and got out of the hot tub game for good.

But the experience had intrigued Suze, who thought that, with a little training, she could do a better job with investments than her broker did. She applied for a job with the same brokerage and got it, "to fill their women's quota," she still insists. She quickly became a hotshot, earning so much money, she sent copies of her paychecks to her amazed mother in Chicago. But she didn't like the brokerage's practice of selling on commission, which forced her to prioritize her company's sales goals over her clients' personal goals. Suze became certified as an independent financial adviser and left the corporate world to open her own office, the Suze Orman Financial Group.

The firm was successful, and Suze, as the principal, was wealthier than she'd ever imagined. She accumulated the trappings she'd always dreamed of: luxury car, gold watch, designer clothes, vacations on private islands. And one day she walked into her office to find she'd been robbed.

None of the office's expensive furniture or computer equipment was missing. What had been taken was far more devastating: the information that drove her entire business. Computer files and software programs, client contact information, financial records—all pilfered in the middle of the night by a (now) former employee.

Although Suze flew into damage control, the next three years were consumed by a financially and emotionally draining lawsuit. The theft had severely impaired the company's ability to function, and Suze's once lavish income dwindled. Refusing to let anyone know her true financial status, she maintained her lifestyle, although it meant burning through her retirement savings, refinancing her house, and maxing out her credit cards. Suze was free-falling through all the irresponsible financial behavior she counseled her clients against.

At a diner one morning, Suze noticed the waitress and the positive attitude she brought to her minimum-wage job—much like the young Suze Orman at that bakery in Berkeley. "I had once been poor, yet had lived with spirit, courageously. Now I was living with the trappings of wealth, but had no money. I was living a lie. I no longer had even the courage to be poor." Suze realized with a shock that, at that moment, this woman was wealthier than she was, both materially and spiritually.

Broke and despondent, Suze embarked on a spiritual quest, exploring Eastern meditation and studying the teachings of the masters. "Slowly, I began to consider all that was happening to me in terms of what God might want to teach me. **If I could view these years as a gift to be unwrapped, I thought, I might find a way to feel enhanced rather than diminished,** grateful rather than bitter."

Suze began to question what all the hard-nosed, number-crunching accountants and brokers of the world had missed: was there a spiritual secret to accumulating wealth? For Suze, it seemed the answer was yes. "The lesson I learned was that my attitude toward money had made me poor and that with that attitude, no amount of money could have made me rich. . . . Money doesn't bring courage, I learned. It's the other way around. Once I took that lesson to heart, I began to rebuild my life."

The spiritual lessons she had learned formed the basis of her counsel to clients. As she struggled to pay off her own debts, she aggressively dissuaded her clients from expensive purchases and credit card charges and encouraged them to put aside almost a year of emergency funds. By now all of her financial advice was spiritually charged, based on her philosophy: "People first, money second, things third."

She put these teachings down in her books: *You've Earned It, Don't Lose It* and *The Nine Steps to Financial Freedom*, which became a runaway best-seller, soon followed by *The Courage to Be Rich* and *The Laws of Money, the Lessons of Life*. She filmed her own specials for PBS, became a regular guest on *Oprah*, snagged columns first in *Self* and then *O* magazine, and set up her own TV show on CNBC. Today the Suze Orman empire brings in several million dollars a year.

But Suze still splits her time between a modest apartment in New York and the same house she bought years ago in Berkeley. Her favorite meal is a diet Coke and Taco Bell. She has a weakness for manicures but never gets polish. She dresses simply, eats frugally, and keeps only two credit cards.

She also donates, on average, 25 percent of her income to charities every year. By now, Suze has lived at each end of the financial spectrum, but she has finally learned to get the maximum return on her spiritual wealth.

Henry Ford

The father of the car culture saw two companies fold before Ford Motor Company revolutionized automotives with the Model T.

At the turn of the new century, Henry Ford had a promising job and a bright future. He had been promoted quickly through the ranks of the Edison Illuminating Company, claiming the title of chief engineer. He had a devoted wife and a newborn son. He also had a secret in the back shed.

Always a "tinkerer," Henry got his start on the farm where he grew up, taking apart watches and inventing machines to make mundane chores easier. His natural gift for all things mechanical eventually won him the prestigious Edison position even with no formal training, but his corporate work didn't satisfy his innate need to create. So he spent all of his spare time in the shed behind his Detroit home. What he did out there was secret, until the day he knocked a hole in the wall and drove out—on the Quadricycle.

The Quadricycle wasn't much more than a seat on bicycle wheels propelled by a combustion engine. And while unrecognizable as a car, that is precisely what it attempted to be. Germany's Karl Benz had patented the world's first automobile in 1886, and as wealthy Americans and Europeans flocked to adopt this new luxury item, thousands of amateur inventors like Henry rushed to launch their own designs.

Henry Ford's business manager later reminisced that Henry was tossed out of so many prospective investors' offices that he broke down one day and sat crying in the street. So Henry, proud papa that he was, began cruising the neighborhood in his prototype, hoping to catch the eye of some curious investor. Instead, he attracted the attention of the *Detroit Journal,* which published an article about him that piqued the interest of a wealthy industrialist and Detroit's mayor. The two came to Henry with an offer: they would back him if he could build a commercial van. He would be chief designer and superintendent, and the firm would be called the Detroit Automobile Company (DAC). It would prove to be one of the first of a long line of Michigan companies to jump into the automotive business.

Henry not only accepted, but gave up a promotion and an ownership stake in Edison to start DAC, encouraged when Edison himself told him,

"Young man, you have the right idea. Keep right at it." But the venture barely got off the ground. While Henry was able to produce a van prototype, he argued vehemently with his backers that the company should instead design and race sports cars in an effort to win press and attention. The investors saw this as an unprofitable distraction and worried that Ford could not deliver on production. With neither side willing to back down, the partnership dissolved only a year later, with an output of less than two dozen cars.

Henry was still insistent on the importance of racing and went forward with the development of a twenty-six-horsepower two-cylinder machine. He even raced it himself, winning an important challenge in 1901. The vehicle outperformed its competition handily and attracted the attention of more investors, who helped him open the Henry Ford Company. However, while Henry's board of directors supported his original foray into auto racing, they too found him overly involved in the sport. Like the DAC board, they also doubted Henry's abilities, so they brought in a consultant, Henry Leland, to advise Henry on design and production. The inevitable creative differences ensued, and as usual, Henry insisted on getting his way. Within a year, Henry left the company, taking $900 and the rights to his own name. Leland was promoted to Ford's position, and the company was soon renamed the Cadillac Motor Company.

When Henry said, **"Failure is the opportunity to begin again more intelligently,"** he was summing up this moment. His racing craze had cost him two companies in two years, and it was time to reconsider. His exposure to the racing scene had him worried that "the public refused to think about the automobile as anything but a fast toy." What captivated Henry's imagination now was the idea that the automobile could be commonly used as private transportation. It could be affordable to the masses, not the privileged few. It could be safer and faster and cheaper—all at the same time. When Henry opened the Ford Motor Company in 1903, he had a vision of the car of the future, and the common man was in the driver's seat.

Out of the more than fifty car companies in the United States at the time, none were mass marketing cars. And while Henry now applied the same focus and doggedness to this dream as he had to his misguided racing strategy, he was still using the same production system as other companies used for luxury cars. He purchased most of the necessary parts from other companies and used teams of skilled mechanics to build individual cars at workstations. Like other companies, he was forced to charge high prices to cover his low productivity.

The prices thrilled Henry's investors, who thought a cheap car could never be more profitable than an expensive one. But Henry continued his crusade, buying out investors who wouldn't support his goal. Henry capitalized on an economic recession to shift the company's money from the standard luxury model to a new, simpler design: the Model N.

With the Model N's moderate success, Henry set to work on the next version, the Model T. He worked on the prototype secretly for two years and found that a revolution in his product required a revolution in production. After learning that French cars used a lighter and safer steel, he brought over a French metallurgist and set up his own steel mill. He began taking over his suppliers, ordering parts to his exact specifications and eliminating the price markup between vendor and buyer.

Henry Ford's most notable innovation was bringing the assembly line to the car factory. He broke up the teams of mechanics, organized workers by job, and brought the job to them via a conveyor belt. This move alone brought the time needed to build one car down from $12\frac{1}{2}$ hours to $1\frac{1}{2}$.

In the first year on the market, 10,000 Model T's were sold—a new record. And just as the demand for cars increased exponentially, so did productivity. Henry built a new factory of unprecedented size, where he constantly tested manufacturing improvements that helped increase production by 100 percent over three years. By 1914, Henry could match his competitors' output using only 13,000 workers; the competition needed 66,350.

The Model T became the most popular car in America, but Henry Ford continued to defy his advisers, not to mention common business practice. As demand rose for the Model T, Henry slashed prices, starting at $800 and dropping to $275. Just as he expected, the public kept buying, and by 1927, he had sold 17 million cars, more than every other brand of car combined. When Henry saw that more and more men were quitting in the face of boredom on the assembly line, he doubled their wages and cut their working day by an hour, knowing their job satisfaction would increase productivity. Despite his stockholders' outrage, that pay raise, Henry later said, was "one of the finest cost-cutting moves we ever made."

Never popular with board members or stockholders, the pay raise and other business practices constantly put Henry at odds with his most important supporters. His driven, unbending nature allowed him to push through untested and unpopular changes, backed by his instinct instead of facts or figures. Henry wouldn't take no for an answer and wouldn't listen to anyone else, which led to his ultimate downfall. Ignoring those who said the Model T's run could not last forever, he refused to make changes to the car's design. He even insisted that it come in any color the customer desired, "as long as it's black." The car was inevitably challenged, first by Chevrolet, then by a host of makes, models, and styles. Henry's abrasive personality cost him some of the best engineers in the business, who left to join competitors. Ford persisted as a company, but with Henry at the helm, it could never maintain its iron grip on the automotive industry.

Henry's stubborn belief in himself led him into personal travails as well. He took an active, vocal, and highly unpopular pacifist stance during World War I and later lost a bid for a U.S. Senate seat. His relationship with his son, and only child, Edsel, became increasingly strained. He was sued by his shareholders for withholding profits. And he embarrassed himself further by publishing a newspaper filled with his anti-Semitic views.

Though irascible, bullheaded, and sometimes simply wrong, no one can deny that Henry Ford's unwavering commitment to his vision changed American life forever. He not only transformed the automotive industry, but also changed the way most industries price their products and pay their workers. Henry's undeviating focus may have outlived its usefulness, but without it, his vision would never have been realized.

Whoopi Goldberg

With a one-woman show that drew on her most painful life experiences, Whoopi finally got her big break.

Whoopi Goldberg—born Caryn Elaine Johnson—grew up in a Manhattan housing project. Her mother, abandoned by her husband, was forced to give up her dream of becoming a doctor and find work as a nurse. But while she had left her own ambitions behind, she refused to let Whoopi accept any limitations, especially regarding her race. "Look, you're black," she would say. "You woke up black this morning; you'll go to bed black tonight. But it doesn't make any difference."

Strict and strong-willed, Emma Johnson insisted on manners and perfect grammar. She nurtured an interest in the arts and, even on their meager budget, exposed Whoopi to New York's cultural treasures: Leonard Bernstein's Young People's Concerts, Joe Papp's Shakespeare in the Park, James Earl Jones in *The Great White Hope*, and Carol Channing in *Hello, Dolly!* Whoopi took acting classes at the Hudson Guild, a community program for inner-city children, and immediately fell in love with the stage. "I could be a princess, a teapot, a rabbit. . . . In a way it's been children's theater ever since."

Whoopi's passion for the stage was outweighed only by her greatest love: old movies. She raced home from school every day and stayed up late every night to watch the glamorous movie stars of old Hollywood. "Movies were my first window to the outside world, and they told me stuff," she later remembered. "They told me I could go anywhere, be whatever I wanted, solve any damn puzzle." The black-and-white fantasy world at first created a uniquely "colorless" escape for the little girl, where people were simply people without any race. But eventually, she came to feel shut out of that fantasy world when she realized that all the black actors were relegated to roles as maids, field hands, or fools. "Movies opened doors to a lot of things for me, but for every one they opened, another one closed."

Unlike her Hollywood idols, Whoopi had neither pale white skin nor silky blond hair. Her strong features made her the butt of jokes, and her shyness and her preference for musicals over Motown made it difficult to fit in. Her struggles in school—due to what would later be diagnosed as dyslexia—led the nuns at her parochial school to suggest she might be mentally retarded. By her freshman year of high school,

Whoopi had had enough of the daily tortures of school. After just a few weeks, she dropped out.

In fact, like many teenagers of the late sixties, she dropped out of society altogether. Whoopi ran away from home, sleeping on the streets and living a counterculture existence of recreational drug use and promiscuous sex. By thirteen, she had terminated her first pregnancy with a coat hanger, and four more abortions followed in as many years. It was only as the sixties turned into the seventies, and friends and icons began overdosing, that Whoopi realized either her life on the streets or her life, period, must come to an end.

Whoopi entered a Manhattan rehab clinic, where she was swept clean of drugs but not of her old fears and insecurities. Afraid of returning to the streets, unwilling to return home, and worried she might otherwise never get married, at eighteen she rushed into marriage with Alvin Martin, one of her drug counselors. She was soon pregnant again, and while she was determined to bear this child, she was equally determined to give an acting career a go.

Alvin discouraged his wife's ambitions, cajoling her to throw out her bohemian style of dress and get a proper desk job. Whoopi, meanwhile, ditched the job interviews he set up to go out on auditions. Fights about money became more frequent. When a friend offered Whoopi and her baby a ride to California, she accepted. The marriage was less than two years old.

Whoopi landed in San Diego with no husband, no high school diploma, no family, and no job. For a while, she worked as a bricklayer, her little girl tagging along on jobs. She installed Sheetrock. She got a scholarship to a beauty school and learned cosmetology, only to practice at a mortuary, where she did the hair and makeup on corpses. Ever the actor, she would even try out characters on her "customers," making them up to look like anyone from Joan Crawford to a punk rocker. But the jobs were rarely permanent or well paid, and for the next few years, she bounced on and off welfare.

Between jobs and welfare checks, Whoopi continued to audition. She eventually found a group of actors at the San Diego Repertory Theater, where she cultivated her dramatic side. She also worked on her comedic skills. In an act inspired by Mike Nichols and Elaine May, a popular comedy duo of the sixties, she paired with a man to do improvised stand-up sets at late-night comedy clubs. One of these gigs earned them an invitation to San Francisco, but when her partner backed out at the last minute, Whoopi went on alone. After her first successful solo performance, she decided to stay.

It was a theater company in Berkeley that gave Whoopi her first big break. They loved her improvisational work and encouraged her to develop it into a one-woman show. In *The Whoopi Goldberg Show*, also called *The Spook Show*, she poured years of struggle into her characters. She introduced audiences to a thirteen-year-old girl who gives herself an abortion with a coat hanger. A highly cultured junkie who drops out of school to live on the streets. A disabled woman who marries partly because she's afraid she'll never find anyone else. A seven-year-old girl who wishes she had blue eyes and blond hair so she could be on TV.

As Whoopi workshopped and performed the piece at various venues, word began to spread, and the San Francisco papers declared the show a hit. Invitations arrived from New York, and in 1984, Whoopi performed *The Spook Show* at an off-off-Broadway theater. A glowing review in the *New York Times* brought in famous actors and directors, including Mike Nichols, director of *The Graduate* and one-half of the Nichols and May team that had inspired Whoopi just a few years before. After the show ended, he rushed backstage to meet the star and offered on the spot to produce the show "anywhere, anytime." Within a year, Whoopi was on Broadway.

With success under her belt, Whoopi could revisit her past with a fresh pair of eyes. "I found that a lot of the people who'd made it tough for me hadn't moved an inch. They were still in the [same] neighborhood. . . . It was a revelation. **Now I feel joy that I was the odd man out. It gave me an out that I didn't recognize at the time."** The difficult experiences she endured lent depth to her pain and resilience to her humor. They created the Whoopi Goldberg known for her brazenness, her insight, and her willingness to speak the unspoken truth.

They also created a hit Broadway show that snowballed into a career. Whoopi's next project and first film role, the lead in Steven Spielberg's *The Color Purple,* earned her an Oscar nomination, and with her supporting role in *Ghost,* she became the second African-American actress ever to win an Academy Award. Today she is known for her work across genres: sitcom star, stand-up comedian, dramatic actress, game-show host, charitable fund-raiser, and children's book writer. And despite the occasional box office bomb, she continues to be—true to type—a survivor.

The Dalai Lama

The Dalai Lama's unjust exile from his homeland propelled him to become a spiritual leader to the world.

Lhamo Thondup, one of the youngest of eight children, was born to poor farmers in a remote region of Tibet. An undistinguished child in a humble land, there was nothing about him to suggest that he would one day become the leader of his nation and one of the world's most eloquent proponents of peace—except for a rash of unusual events surrounding the little boy's birth.

His father had been bedridden until Lhamo Thondup was born, at which point he became mysteriously well overnight. The family noticed that the baby insisted on sitting at the head of the table. As he grew older, he would pack a small bag and announce, "I'm going to Lhasa!" the seat of the great Dalai Lama, the holiest of political and religious leaders in Tibetan Buddhism. Lhamo Thondup's family attributed his unusual behavior to his rambunctious personality.

But when one day a group of travelers stopped at the house and asked for shelter for the night, the two-year-old went directly to a servant with the group and announced excitedly, "Sera Lama!" The little boy saw what no one else could: the servant was, in fact, a great monk, or lama, who was from the prestigious Sera monastery. He was dressed in disguise as part of what was now revealed to be a search party.

Buddhists believe that the Dalai Lama is the reincarnation of every Dalai Lama who came before him, with a spiritual ancestry that traces all the way back to Siddartha, the original Buddha and founder of the religion. The thirteenth Dalai Lama had recently died, and this group had followed signs from their oracles to the little boy's house in search of the Dalai Lama's reincarnation. They now laid out a selection of personal items, some of which had been the previous Dalai Lama's. Lhamo Thondup easily picked out his predecessor's belongings, insisting, "It's mine! It's mine!"

The little boy, soon installed as the fourteenth Dalai Lama, left his family behind to spend the next twenty years studying to be a monk and, eventually, his people's leader. It was an extremely sheltered life, spent in the company of tutors and fellow monks, living exclusively in monasteries. Strict protocol shielded him from any commoners.

When the Dalai Lama was fifteen, soldiers from neighboring Communist China raided an outlying Tibetan post. Tibetans knew that their army of 8,500 would be no deterrent to China's army of 80,000. The Dalai Lama received a visit from his brother, also a monk, soon afterward. He reported that his monastery had been overrun by Chinese Communists who were trying to indoctrinate the monks in their propaganda. He had personally been ordered to visit the Dalai Lama and, if he could not convince him to accept Chinese rule, to kill him.

In the midst of this chaos, the scared and sheltered fifteen-year-old became officially enthroned as the Dalai Lama, assuming all powers as the lay leader of Tibet. As throngs of Chinese soldiers entered the country, reports poured in of abuses at their hands. The soldiers had begun seizing land and property and redistributing it among the Chinese officials who followed. Far worse were stories of the brutalities suffered by common peasants, though the brunt of China's wrath seemed reserved for religious figures. In an effort to discredit the Buddhist religion, the Chinese forced monks and nuns to publicly break their vows of celibacy and to kill small animals. Some were made to kill other people, and almost all were detained in concentration camps. Eventually all religion would be banned in Tibet.

The young Dalai Lama sent ambassadors to Great Britain and the United States to ask them to intervene on Tibet's behalf. Both sent back the ambassadors empty-handed, essentially agreeing that China had some authority over Tibet. With none of the world's great powers willing to support his cause, the Dalai Lama sent a team to China to negotiate peaceful and fair terms for coexistence. He later heard on the radio that the team had signed a full surrender.

Knowing the deal must have been struck at gunpoint, the Dalai Lama realized that Tibet had no choice but to go along with the surrender. He traveled to China and spent months there securing audiences with Chinese officials, including Mao Tse-tung, to plead for his country's independence. But he was young and naive, and the officials who met with him plied him with empty promises and outright lies.

Upon his return to Tibet, the Dalai Lama found the situation unraveling. The Chinese crushed any sign of rebellion, using aircraft fire on small villages and subjecting resisters to medieval punishment, including crucifixion and disembowelment. When the Dalai Lama was invited to a Chinese event but prohibited from bringing his bodyguards, assassination seemed inevitable. The exalted leader slipped out of the country, disguised as a low-ranking soldier. The two-week journey to India, on foot and by donkey, took the Dalai Lama and his entourage through a blizzard, suffering dysentery the whole way.

India awarded the group political asylum, and while the move had been traumatic, the Dalai Lama found that he was suddenly afforded a freedom he had never known. In exile, he was able to publicly denounce the Chinese invasion without fear of reprisal. But he was also able to do away with the restrictive protocol that had surrounded him since childhood. This brought him in closer contact with people of all kinds, especially the refugees fleeing Tibet, with their stories of courage in the face of horrific abuses. He convinced the Indian government to extend asylum to these refugees, securing funds for their shelter and education.

The newfound access to a range of people and opinions profoundly shaped the Dalai Lama. Angered by China's totalitarian approach and with a new respect for the people's will, the Dalai Lama established a Tibetan government-in-exile and restructured it to reflect modern-day democratic models. In a change from a previous regime that was mostly appointed, members of his parliament are now freely elected by the Tibetan people in exile, and the Dalai Lama has declared that once Tibet regains independence, he will not hold political office, returning to a religious capacity only.

Since that frightened teenager took power, the Dalai Lama has become a seasoned politician. He has now traveled to forty-six countries to raise awareness of his country's plight—quite a change from a childhood restricted to monastery halls. After his first failures to win the support of Great Britain and the United States, he successfully lobbied the United Nations to approve a resolution demanding that China respect Tibet's right to self-determination. He also initiated a plan to restore self-rule and human rights, with the stipulation that this must be achieved peacefully, without the use of force.

A full schedule of diplomacy does not stop the Dalai Lama from speaking and writing on Buddhist philosophy, reaching people of all faiths and nations. His teachings personalize his political views by urging people to cultivate peace and forgiveness in the human heart. He also counsels on the wisdom found in tragedy. In *The Dalai Lama's Book of Wisdom*, he wrote: "Because of [a] tragic experience you become more realistic, you become closer to reality. With the power of investigation, **the tragic experience may make you stronger** and increase your self-confidence and self-reliance. The unfortunate event can be a source of inner strength."

Despite the horrors inflicted by Chinese rule, peaceful negotiation has always been the cornerstone of the Dalai Lama's political philosophy and his religious teachings. When he was awarded the Nobel Peace Prize in 1989, the award recognized not just his work on behalf of oppressed Tibetans, but his efforts to promote peace and reconciliation throughout the world, both between nations and between neighbors. In his acceptance speech, he said, "With truth, courage, and determination as our weapons, Tibet will be liberated." But his greater message? So will we all.

Susan B. Anthony

A lifetime of being silenced and ignored drove Susan to fight for the right to vote.

At a well-attended Sons of Temperance meeting in 1852, Susan B. Anthony, a regular contributor at women's temperance meetings, stood to speak. For years, she had been an active proponent of temperance, the reform movement to ban alcohol in the United States. Like other female supporters, Susan was especially concerned for fellow women who had no escape from alcoholic husbands who abused or abandoned them. But these concerns would not be addressed that night. Susan was promptly informed that "the sisters were not invited there to speak but to listen and learn."

Susan was not used to being silenced. She had been born into a Massachusetts Quaker family known for embracing progressive issues and equality for women. Her father, a mill owner and later a farmer, ensured that his children—both sons and daughters—received a quality education. When Susan's teacher at the local one-room schoolhouse refused to show her how to do long division, Mr. Anthony opened his own school and hired a highly educated young woman to teach her male and female students the same curriculum, including physical education—a rarity for young girls at the time. Susan herself had became a headmistress at a girls' school and encouraged her charges to think and speak for themselves.

Now, silenced at a meeting run by men, Susan was justly infuriated, and boycotted the group. She quickly founded a rival organization for women's involvement in temperance reform, taking care to encourage men's participation as well. The newly established Woman's State Temperance Society of New York began holding their own meetings and set up their own convention, where Susan B. Anthony was elected secretary and her closest friend and fellow activist, Elizabeth Cady Stanton, was elected president.

Anthony and Stanton's inclusive agenda proved so successful that by the group's second convention, men made up a majority of the membership. But their inclusion had an unforeseen consequence: the pair were voted out of the party's leadership because of their strongly held beliefs on women's rights, especially a woman's right to divorce her abusive husband.

Anthony and Stanton tried to build ties with other women's temperance groups around the country and found that, by and large, most had disintegrated. Since working women made very little money and married women had no rights to theirs, it was next to impossible for women to fund and run any organization without a man's financial backing. Women could only hope to join a men's organization, where they would have no voice and no leadership role.

These setbacks led Susan to a painful but important realization. Despite her hard work, it became clear that women's temperance groups—and abolitionist and other social reform groups—would never play more than a supporting role to the men's. Liquor laws were an important cause, but until women had an equal place at the table, they would be unable to effect any real or lasting societal change. The most important fight facing women was for their own equal rights.

Anthony and Stanton shifted their focus and joined forces to battle for the New York Married Women's Property Bill, a cause close to Susan's heart. She remembered how, when her father's mill went bankrupt, she watched as creditors sold off her mother's possessions—even those that her mother owned before her wedding—as her father's own holdings.

Everything Susan's mother owned had legally become her husband's property the day they married.

Susan worked tirelessly to secure property and guardianship rights for married women, who had no say over their earnings, their possessions, or even their children's upbringing. Susan spoke to audiences about the young innkeeper's wife she had met on her lecturing tour, who balanced a baby on her hip while preparing a filling meal and tending to her guests in a clean and well-appointed inn. The next morning, the young mother's husband, who had sat in the bar all night drinking with his pals, pocketed Susan's money as she paid for her stay. Nothing illustrated more for Susan the economic injustice of the current system. It took six years to pass the bill, but in 1860, married women in the state of New York gained the right to own property, sign contracts, keep their own earnings, and share legal rights over their children.

With greater economic rights secured, Susan turned her sights on political equality. As a committed abolitionist, she was thrilled with the passage of the Emancipation Proclamation and culled from her own ranks of supporters 400,000 signatures for the passage of the Thirteenth Amendment, which guaranteed freedom for African Americans. She then worked to include women in the Fourteenth and Fifteenth Amendments—which gave black men full citizens' rights—expecting the women's movement's loyalty to abolition to be appreciated and repaid through reciprocal support from men's groups. Almost all of her male abolitionist colleagues—all close friends and longtime supporters—rejected her strategy, saying African-American men must take precedence and that women must wait their turn.

Susan knew then that it had been a mistake to shift her movement's focus from equal rights for all to emancipation for some. As her friend Elizabeth Cady Stanton said, "If the leaders in the . . . abolition camps could deceive us, whom could we trust?"

With no one to depend on but themselves, Stanton and Anthony founded a new political organization, the National Woman Suffrage Association. The group would be led by women and be committed to women, with one unwavering focus: to secure American women the right to vote. Susan called universal suffrage "the solution to everything," for it was only with true government representation that women would be able to right society's wrongs.

Never afraid to court controversy, Susan organized a drive to vote illegally in the 1872 presidential election, hoping to be arrested and tried and ultimately to appeal the voting laws' constitutionality to the Supreme Court. When Susan was brought to trial, the judge refused to let her testify, ruling that she was "incompetent, as a woman, to speak for herself." Although it was a jury trial, the judge dismissed the jurors before deliberations and found Susan guilty himself. The judge also refused to jail her, knowing this would gain sympathy for her cause and allow her to appeal to the Supreme Court. The trial was a boon for public opinion, since it raised support even from Susan's opponents, who thought the sham trial was patently unfair. But it also showed Susan that without a constitutional amendment, establishing woman suffrage would be impossible.

Susan spent the rest of her life pushing the woman suffrage agenda forward. Even as states in the western territories gave women the vote, Susan stayed focused, trying to build a critical mass behind a constitutional amendment. Susan worked almost right up to her death, writing that she wanted to "die in the harness" rather than fade away. In her last speech, she predicted that suffrage was at hand and confidently declared, **"Failure is impossible."** She died two weeks later at the age of eighty-six, saying from her deathbed, "Remember that the only fear you need have is the fear of not standing by the thing you believe to be right."

In the next twelve years, at least partial suffrage had spread to twenty-nine states, and in 1920—one hundred years after Susan B. Anthony's birth—the United States finally passed the Nineteenth Amendment: "The right of citizens of the United States to vote shall not be denied or abridged by the United States or by any State on account of sex." The political organization Susan founded had become the League of Women Voters. And in 1979, the woman who had fought to secure women equal economic rights became the first woman to appear on an American coin: the Susan B. Anthony dollar.

John Grisham

It took rejection letters from sixteen agents and more than thirty publishing houses to get this best-selling author's first book into print.

Despite over 100 million copies of his books in print in the United States alone, John Grisham "never dreamed of being a writer." Born to an undistinguished Arkansas family with no particular literary aspirations, John has admitted, "I was never really a bookworm," favoring Dr. Seuss and the Hardy Boys in his youth.

A brief interest in the novels of John Steinbeck was ultimately displaced by his true love: baseball. With an eye on the majors, John focused all of his time and attention on the field and went to Mississippi State University to play at the college level. But watching a college game one day, he reconsidered his prospects: "It dawned on me that the players I was watching, though my age, also had a very slight chance of playing pro ball. I decided we were in the same boat. And it was best to start studying for a change."

John graduated from Mississippi State with an accounting degree, then moved on to the University of Mississippi law school. For the next decade, he practiced law in the town of Southaven, Mississippi, just over the state border from Memphis. His firm brought in mostly small-time criminal defendants and personal injury cases. Looking for more of a challenge, he ran for and was elected to the state House of Representatives.

As a legislator, John continued his law practice, and the more time he spent in law, the more he was inspired by the stories he heard. The case of a twelve-year-old rape victim in particular captured his attention. He found himself wondering: what would happen if her father took the law into his own hands and avenged her assault? With this question in mind, John began to jot down ideas, then plot outlines. Pretty soon, he was writing.

A sixty- to eighty-hour workweek as a state representative didn't leave much time for amateur scribblings. But John persisted, getting up every morning at five A.M. to fit in an hour of writing. At this plodding rate, it took three years to finish his novel. He named it *A Time to Kill*.

With a completed manuscript and no small sense of accomplishment, John turned to his next arduous task: getting an agent. He sent a polite letter, including his manuscript for review. He got a rejection letter in return. Another letter. Another rejection. In the end, sixteen agents rejected his novel and him as a client. And once he did sign with an agent, the rejection merry-go-round started up again. The novel was submitted to what John now remembers as "thirty-something" publishing houses, and thirty-something editors turned it down.

But one editor liked what he saw—and he would know. Bill Thompson from Wynwood Press was the editor who discovered Stephen King. He gave *A Time to Kill* a limited 5,000-book run and John a $15,000 advance. John bought 1,000 copies to sell himself and created his own self-styled book tour, traveling the mid-South in his old Volvo to do book signings with perhaps a dozen people in attendance.

Neither the book nor the tour made John Grisham a runaway best-selling author. While John sold a few books, the tour did not net much more than a few new friendships with local bookstore owners. The limited run was not extended.

But John had been bitten with the writing bug, and the day after he finished *A Time to Kill*, he started his second novel: a thriller about a hot-shot young lawyer who gets seduced by a flashy but corrupt Memphis law firm. Not long after *The Firm* finally made it to his agent's desk, John was surprised to find out that it had been purchased for $600,000—not by a publishing house, but by Paramount Pictures. The story was deemed prime blockbuster material, perfect for a major star like, say, Tom Cruise. The high-stakes deal piqued the interest of New York's biggest publishing houses, many of whom had passed on John's first novel. One of New York's most prestigious publishers, Doubleday, matched Paramount's offer. Once published, *The Firm* spent forty-seven weeks on the *New York Times* best-seller list and became the best-selling novel of 1991.

Now, with ten best-sellers under his belt and his law career set aside, John has never regretted the years he spent before the bar, reflecting, "I seriously doubt I would ever have written the first story had I not been a lawyer." But his eventual success sprang from his desire to reinvent the profession that had become stale: "I never planned to write books; it was not something I ever thought about. I thought I'd be a lawyer for the rest of my life. . . . **Success a lot of times depends on whether you make a change and try something that you hadn't planned."**

Maya Angelou

In a childhood filled with violence, prejudice, and self-imposed silence, the writer discovered her voice.

When a scared little black girl and her brother stepped off the train in Depression-era Stamps, Arkansas, they had no way of knowing they were entering the only haven they would know in their young lives. Maya Angelou, born Marguerite Johnson, was sent away by her parents after their divorce to live with her father's mother. Her grandmother, Momma, was the only African-American store owner in a segregated southern town, and while the family was poor, at times they were actually more prosperous than some local whites.

Momma was a strict but devoted authority figure who pushed the children to excel in school and held them to higher expectations than their peers. Awkward-looking in a family that was "handsome to a point of pain" and feeling lost after her parents' abandonment, Maya soaked up this loving discipline. It was a vital life raft in the sea of indignities she endured as a young black girl in the segregated South. Like most girls her age, she wore hand-medowns from white ladies and dreamed of the day when she would wake up and find herself graced with blond hair and blue eyes. During a brief stint as a maid, she found her name changed to "Mary" by an employer who found Marguerite "too long." She was refused urgent care from a dentist who told her grandmother, "I'd rather stick my hand in a dog's mouth than in a nigger's."

While none of these slights were out of the ordinary for the time, Maya could not help but be galled at how accepted such behavior had become. "If growing up is painful for the Southern Black girl," she wrote, "being aware of her displacement is the rust on the razor that threatens the throat. It is an unnecessary insult."

In the midst of these affronts, Maya won some small successes. She loved reading with a passion and fell in love with classics like Shakespeare and Poe, while discovering African-American poets like Paul Laurence Dunbar. Maya established herself as a good student, and her grandmother's position in town won her respect in the community. But while she loved the time spent with her grandmother, she still wondered why her parents had no room for her. So when the opportunity arose for Maya and her brother, Bailey, to join their mother in St. Louis, they took it.

In St. Louis, Maya and Bailey experienced the "big city" in all its excitement: the new foods, the sights and sounds, the ethnic diversity, the fun of meeting their mother's extended family. But it was also here that Maya experienced the greatest trauma of her eight years and many to come: her mother's boyfriend raped her.

She was sworn to keep the crime a secret, but when her brother guessed, she revealed her attacker's name. He was arrested and put on trial, where Maya's testimony sentenced him to prison. Maya's mother's family had political connections, and it was most likely they who arranged to have him released that day and beaten to death on the street.

When the news of her attacker's death reached Maya, she was shocked into silence. "If I talked to anyone else," she worried, "that person might die, too. Just my breath, carrying my words out, might poison people and they'd curl up and die." There was only one solution. "I had to stop talking."

For the next five years, Maya didn't speak. Her mother's family soon labeled her behavior insolence and sent her and Bailey back to live with her grandmother in Arkansas. But while her grandmother's nurturing and the town's sleepiness seemed like a respite, Maya felt suffocated under the weight of the sins she had taken on. Her once-quick mind slowed as she began forgetting familiar names and faces. Sounds seemed fuzzy. Colors seemed faded. Maya could not shake the idea that she might slowly be going insane.

On one of these muted, quiet days at the store, Maya's savior entered. Mrs. Flowers was a schoolteacher who had heard of Maya's studious muteness. She asked the girl to come to her house, where she took books off the shelf and began to read aloud. The books were familiar to Maya—she had read many of them before. But she had never heard the beauty of the words spoken aloud. "It was the best of times, it was the worst of times," read Mrs. Flowers, and Maya sat enraptured. Mrs. Flowers insisted that Maya take home books and read them aloud—and that she return each week with a poem memorized to recite.

Maya was thrilled to be singled out for Mrs. Flowers's attention. It was the first time she felt truly "liked, and what a difference it made. I was respected not as Mrs. Henderson's grandchild or Bailey's sister but for just being Marguerite Johnson." She returned over the weeks with poems and snippets of prose. She read aloud and savored the words in her mouth, in the air. Books had always been her escape—the trusted, private pathway out of a life of pain and dejection. But now they became her light, guiding her reentry into life, helping her to find joy in the midst of the pain.

Books would always be Maya Angelou's touchstone. As a writer, she would capture all the grim, joyous, and challenging experiences of her life in the pages of her poetry and memories. In her own words, **"I can be changed by what happens to me. I refuse to be reduced by it."** Maya's experiences did not deflate her: they became the opportunity to reinvent herself and create her art. Her life's adventures—a teenage pregnancy; work as a dancer, an actress, and a one-time madam; multiple failed marriages; a move to Ghana; civil rights demonstrations with Dr. Martin Luther King, Jr.—all became the subject of the many volumes of her best-selling memoirs.

Today, Maya Angelou is known as a poet, a historian, an author, an actress, a playwright, a civil rights activist, a producer, and a director. She has taught at the University of Ghana and holds an endowed chair at Wake Forest University. She has been nominated for a Pulitzer Prize, a Tony, and an Emmy Award. She has written ten best-sellers and wrote and delivered a poem commissioned by Bill Clinton at his 1993 presidential inauguration. Her writing has come to symbolize her willingness to reinvent her life—with all of her pains and triumphs—as art and to use her art to celebrate life itself.

Winston Churchill

England's most stubborn leader led the country through World War II by tenaciously holding to lessons learned from earlier mistakes.

According to popular mythology, Winston Churchill returned to his alma mater, the Harrow School, in wartime to deliver the commencement address. The prime minister famously intoned the words that roused the British: **"Never give up. Never give up. Never give up."**

It was a rallying cry not just for the graduates or even the shaken British people, but for Winston's entire life. Distinguished by his stubbornness from an early age, it was just this determination that led to a career filled with as many detours as triumphs. But his determination persisted through the down times, and his ability to come back from defeat ultimately prepared him for his highest calling.

Young Winston inherited an illustrious pedigree and all the expectations that accompanied it. The oldest son of Lord Randolph

Henry Spencer Churchill, a leader of the House of Commons, and Jennie Jerome, the beautiful daughter of a New York tycoon, Winston spent his childhood in the cold and splendid halls of Blenheim Palace, his family's estate. His parents had little time for him, and his only source of love and affection was his nanny, whose picture he kept by his bedside until the day he died.

The family suspected Winston would never live up to his family name. He was short and stubborn and had difficulty making friends. He was plagued by a speech impediment. He did not distinguish himself at Harrow, since he hated the classical curriculum. His faltering academic record made a shining political career unlikely, so his father sent him to Sandhurst, the military academy, where it took Winston three tries to pass the entrance exam.

He took surprisingly well to the military and distinguished himself throughout his twenties by his bravery under attack. He also built a reputation for himself as a journalist by writing books and articles on the exotic locales he visited on maneuvers. On the strength of a particularly courageous performance in the Boer War in South Africa, he ran for Parliament on the Conservative Party ticket—his father's own—when he returned home. He lost, but two years later, he ran again and claimed his seat.

Winston rose quickly through the political ranks, winning Cabinet posts even while bouncing between political parties. His military background eventually gained him the position of First Lord of the Admiralty, where his views were so well respected he won the largest naval appropriation in British history. Winston immediately put it to use to rebuild the British Navy in anticipation of what he rightly perceived to be a looming German threat.

Unfortunately, his military expertise would soon fail him. In World War I, Winston Churchill became a loud and insistent proponent of a naval campaign to open the Dardanelles Strait in Turkey. The operations failed, and fellow Cabinet members backed away from the plan, letting Winston take the fall. In the greatest career reversal of his life, he was demoted to a lower position but given leadership over a land campaign in the same region—one which resulted in catastrophic losses in Gallipoli. This time, Winston resigned and volunteered for active duty on the French front.

This display of gallantry eventually won over his supporters, and he returned to a succession of Cabinet posts at the end of the war. But his dogged insistence on a return to the Dardanelles in 1922 lost what little backing he had left. On the eve of an important election, Winston was stricken with appendicitis and was not able to campaign his constituencies until two days before the election. He was defeated by over 10,000 votes.

Over the next decade, Winston found himself in and out of the House of Commons under a number of party banners. By 1931, his outspoken views and lack of diplomacy had alienated every party, and no one wanted to claim him. With another election lost, he stepped down from the political scene.

Yet Winston still could not quiet his outspoken political views. He was especially concerned about the rising star of Germany's new leader, Adolf Hitler. Suspecting him to be the greatest threat to democracy since Bolshevik Russia, Winston Churchill soon became the most vocal opponent of England's appeasement policy. His views were unpopular, and while he persistently met with government leaders and spoke openly about the looming German threat, the current administration distanced themselves from him. Winston continued his work by cultivating a select group of peers who supported his stance. He effectively created his own makeshift intelligence organization, utilizing the documents secretly procured by his supporters.

As Germany aggressively pursued its neighbors, the British public grew more dissatisfied with the current prime minister's attempts to pacify the German dictator. On September 3, 1939, the day Britain declared war on Germany, Prime Minister Neville Chamberlain reappointed Winston Churchill to his original post as Lord of the Admiralty. By 1940, he was elected prime minister.

As he said in his own words, Winston felt his whole life "had been but a preparation for this hour and for this trial, and I was sure I should not fail." Every heretofore personal and professional failing now came together to form the foundation of Winston's triumph. The stubborn, sometimes arrogant, approach he used had never won him any friends, but it provided the country with the solid leadership it needed in uncertain times. He had never shaken the speech impediment of his youth, which required him to carefully write, rewrite, and rehearse every public speech. These exquisitely crafted speeches roused the British to their "finest hour" and have since gone down as perhaps the most influential in history. President Kennedy best captured it when he said, "He mobilized the English language and sent it into battle."

Even the Dardanelles, the beginning of Winston's professional unraveling, played an important role in the Allied European strategy. Having learned the risk of premature intervention from the earlier military debacle, he lobbied American generals Marshall and Eisenhower to hold off their attacks on the Continent until they were assured of victory. And when their combined forces invaded Normandy on D Day, Winston was dissuaded from accompanying the warships only by a personal appeal from King George VI.

Winston Churchill is still given the lion's share of credit behind the Allied victory in World War II, as his focused and determined leadership brought together the crucial triumvirate of the United States, Russia, and England. Yet just months after Germany's surrender, he was voted out of office by an English populace dissatisfied with Conservative Party leadership. The most challenging aspects of his personality were ideal for wartime, they seemed to say, but not for peace.

Although Winston Churchill regained the prime minister seat in 1951, he resigned four years later in ailing health and never regained his popularity—a fitting end to a fickle career. Winston's story illustrates the necessity and limits of persistence in the face of failure, as well as victory. But to him, perhaps persistence *was* victory. For as he said: "Success is never final. Failure is never fatal. It is courage that counts."

Malcolm X

The civil rights leader escaped his demons and discovered his purpose while in prison on a petty burglary charge.

In notes on a draft of the autobiography he dictated to Alex Haley, Malcolm X wrote: **"Children have a lesson adults should learn, to not be ashamed of failing, but to get up and try again."** And in his childhood, Malcolm—born Malcolm Little—was an unwilling eyewitness to crippling and sometimes crushing setbacks.

Malcolm grew up in a world defined by racial tension, and his childhood was one of a steady decline under the weight of prejudice, poverty, and personal tragedy. Living in small, overwhelmingly white Midwestern towns, his father, a traveling preacher, was often threatened for his active support of Marcus Garvey and the black nationalist movement. The family endured midnight visits from the Klan and watched their house burn to the ground while white authorities stood by. Racial violence even found its way into Malcolm's father's stormy marriage to his mother, a light-skinned woman who could pass for white. Malcolm remembered color sparking not only his parents' fights, but also the harshness of their treatment of their eight children, who ranged in color.

When Malcolm was six, his father died of mysterious injuries, probably inflicted by hostile whites who beat him and then threw him in front of a streetcar. The family had always been financially unstable, but when the life insurance company contested payment, they quickly slid into poverty. It did not take long for his mother to succumb to grief and distress. When Malcolm turned twelve, she had a nervous breakdown and remained in the state mental hospital for the majority of her life.

After their mother's breakdown, Malcolm and his siblings were separated and moved to foster care. Malcolm began getting into trouble at school and was sent to a detention home. Here, he was surprised to find the most stable home environment he'd ever encountered. He started applying himself at school. His grades rose to the top of the class. To his own surprise, he was even elected class president.

But no matter what success he found, he continued to be dogged by racism. As the only black student in school, Malcolm was continually singled out and mocked by teachers and students alike. In American history class, his teacher covered the history of African Americans in one paragraph and a racist joke. Malcolm was most devastated by the whites who claimed to look out for his best interests. When his favorite teacher asked him what he wanted to be when he grew up, he answered, "A lawyer," only to be told to find a "useful" skill, like carpentry. Even the loving guardians at his detention home regularly used racial slurs around him.

At the end of eighth grade, the discouraged Malcolm quit school and left for Boston to visit his half-sister. Lured by the sights and sounds of the big city, he was determined to stay and got hired as a shoeshine boy at the Roseland Ballroom, where he quickly became the go-to man for drugs and prostitutes. By the time he was seventeen, he had graduated to the job of full-time street hustler and had moved to Harlem, working directly for local pimps and drug dealers and then dealing himself. He also became a regular user and ultimately an addict.

Looking for the next big score, Malcolm formed a burglary ring back in Boston with a friend, an upper-class white girl, and her sister. The team used the girl's access to wealthy houses to make nighttime raids, but Malcolm was caught trying to fence the goods. Malcolm and his friend were charged and got the maximum sentence: eight to ten years.

At twenty-one, Malcolm Little found himself in one of the only two places he'd ever expected to end up: in jail or in the grave. His rebelliousness extended even to the prison facilities in Charlestown, Massachusetts, where he quickly earned the nickname "Satan" for his tendency to lash out at anyone and everyone. He continued his drug habit behind bars with whatever narcotics he could find and engaged in his own brand of sullen disobedience: dropping his tray in the cafeteria, talking back to guards, pretending to forget his prison number. He was known for staying up all night in his cell, preaching diatribes against the Bible and God.

But in the license plate shop, Malcolm met a fellow inmate known as Bimbi. A longtime petty thief, Bimbi was unlike any white or black man Malcolm had ever known. Well read, pensive, and studious, he would talk to inmates about his favorite topics: history and religion. Malcolm later reflected, "What fascinated me with him most of all was that he was the first man I had ever seen command total respect . . . with his words." He was also the only person Malcolm had ever known who seemed to believe in him, telling him bluntly, "You have some brains, if you'd use them." Bimbi encouraged Malcolm to follow his own example and take advantage of the prison correspondence courses and the library.

Malcolm soon began a correspondence course in English. Years on the street, away from school, had rendered him virtually illiterate and his writing illegible. Intrigued by Bimbi's lectures on word derivation, he started reading the dictionary, one page a day, beginning with "aardvark," and committing the words to memory.

His newfound interest in study helped to quell his more rebellious instincts, and after a year, Malcolm was transferred to Norfolk Prison Colony, an experimental prison model designed to rehabilitate the prisoner. The facility boasted a university-level library and visiting lectures from Harvard professors. Here, Malcolm read deeply into world history, philosophy, and religion. He read *Uncle Tom's Cabin* and nineteenth-century abolitionist literature. He even studied the genetic findings of Gregor Mendel and Charles Darwin. Malcolm always credited his prison studies with his later activism. When a reporter asked him his alma mater, he answered, "Books."

Malcolm joined the prison debating team, where he polished the skills that would prove to be most valuable to him: how to speak publicly and sway a crowd to his point of view. More important, he began using the platform to forward the philosophy that had captivated his thinking: the teachings of Elijah Muhammad, head of the Nation of Islam.

Perhaps the most significant outcome of Malcolm's incarceration was that it made him quite literally a captive audience for the Nation of Islam. Introduced to the group by his siblings who had become converts, Malcolm found that the organization's teachings on black empowerment rang true with everything he had experienced. And for a man who had led a life of rebellion, he found himself strangely intrigued by Islam's message of submission. For the first time in his life, in the darkness of his cell, he got down on his hands and knees and prayed to Allah. Soon he was actively working to convert his fellow convicts.

Malcolm was released early and headed to Detroit, where he became Elijah Muhammad's protégé. He had his name legally changed to "Malcolm X," rejecting his original last name as a slaveholder's legacy. He quickly rose to become a minister of the organization and ultimately its primary spokesman. By the time he was assassinated in 1965, he had made the Nation of Islam a household name and an important presence in the civil rights struggle. He had almost single-handedly increased their rolls from 400 to 40,000 members.

Today, Malcolm X is remembered as the opposite of everything he was when he entered prison. Once a petty hustler, he became a leader for his race. Once a man weakened by vice, he became a moral example for his followers. Once an atheist, he became this country's most famous and influential Muslim. It was not without a little irony that Malcolm later reflected, "I don't think anybody ever got more out of going to prison than I did."

Ruth Bader Ginsburg

**Faced with sexism in her own workplace, she paved her way
to the Supreme Court by fighting for the rights of all women.**

With an unrivaled academic record and work ethic, Ruth Bader
Ginsburg seemed almost too talented for failure. Perhaps if she had
been born thirty years later, she wouldn't have had to confront the
sexism that threatened to derail her career. But without this constant threat, she wouldn't have been forced to fight for her own
equal rights or for those of all women. And without this fight, she
might never have earned her seat on the Supreme Court.

Ruth was born in 1933 in Brooklyn to Jews who had fled religious
persecution in Central Europe and Russia. While her father worked
first as a furrier and then a haberdasher, both parents had greater
ambitions for their only child. Ruth's mother made sure to challenge her intellectually curious daughter with frequent trips to the
library and insisted on saving what little money she could for college. Unfortunately, she was never able to see her daughter achieve
this dream—she died the day before Ruth's high school graduation.

Ruth continued on to Cornell, where she made Phi Beta Kappa and graduated as the top woman in her class. It was also where she met her future husband, Martin Ginsburg, whom she married after graduation and followed to Fort Sill, Oklahoma, while Martin served on the army base. Pregnant and hoping to supplement Martin's army pay, Ruth got a job but was surprised to find her stellar academic career didn't carry much weight. Her salary was reduced three levels below the original offer because she was pregnant.

When Martin was accepted to Harvard Law School, Ruth traveled to Cambridge, this time with baby in tow. She considered submitting an application herself and sought her father-in-law's advice. "If you don't want to go to law school, you have the best excuse in the world, and nobody will think the less of you," he said. "But if you really want to be a lawyer, **you will stop feeling sorry for yourself, and you will find a way."** That year, she applied and was accepted to Harvard Law, only to be scolded by a law school dean for wasting a coveted spot at a time when law firms would never hire women. Determined to prove her right to the classroom, Ruth earned impeccable grades and soon made the *Law Review*.

But on the heels of Ruth's triumph came tragedy. In Martin's last year of law school, he was diagnosed with a particularly lethal kind of cancer. While he was incapacitated with radiation therapy, Ruth tended to his health, all the while taking care of their child, keeping up with her classes, and covering the classes Martin missed. She followed his classes so diligently that, after his recovery, he actually graduated on time and was offered a job with a prestigious New York law firm.

The job offer necessitated another move, and Ruth transferred her credits to Columbia, where she finished out her last year of law school as editor of the *Columbia Law Review* and tied for first in her class. But after all the struggle and successes, it seemed as if the Harvard Law dean had been right all along: no New York law firm would hire her. She applied for a prestigious clerkship with Supreme Court justice Felix Frankfurter. Although he called her "scary smart," he refused to even interview her. Ruth later sympathized with her reluctant employers; maybe hiring "a woman, a Jew, and a mother to boot" was a bit too much for them to handle in the late 1950s.

A Columbia professor stepped in to help Ruth secure a position. He contacted Edmund L. Palmieri, a district court judge known for his more progressive attitudes. Even he only agreed to hire Ruth if her professor promised to secure an unmarried male graduate to stand on call, if needed.

Ruth eventually moved into academia, where she would spend a large part of her career. As only the second woman to join the Rutgers University faculty, she found herself hiding her second pregnancy under oversized clothes in fear of losing her nontenured position.

It was around this time that Ruth first read Simone de Beauvoir's classic feminist book *The Second Sex*. Ruth finally saw the discrimination she had faced not as her own personal setbacks, but as a sign of the pervasive double standard that women encountered every day throughout society. With this realization, Ruth joined forces with the American Civil Liberty Union (ACLU) Women's Rights Project to, in her words, "help advance the vibrant idea of the equal stature and dignity of men and women as a matter of constitutional principle." She was convinced that women would achieve equality only with the full support of the U.S. judicial system. But equal rights for women were only part of the picture. Ruth was more committed to gender equity, explaining, "It is not *women's* liberation. It is women's *and men's* liberation."

With the ACLU, she advanced sex discrimination cases that hit very close to home, like the one on behalf of schoolteachers who were forced to forfeit their jobs when they became pregnant. She helped overturn laws that allowed women to be replaced by men as administrators of estates. She also won Social Security benefits for a widowed father who wanted to stay home and raise his child, challenging the court's assumption that only a mother could be a stay-at-home parent. As head of the Women's Rights Project, Ruth argued six cases before the U.S. Supreme Court. She won five.

Her groundbreaking work in gender equity law won Ruth the first tenured law position for a woman at her alma mater, Columbia. Her work also caught the eye of President Jimmy Carter, who named her a judge to the U.S. Court of Appeals for the District of Columbia Circuit. The new job required her to move to Washington, D.C. This time, Martin followed *her*.

Thirteen years later, with a career that fought for women's rights for three decades on both sides of the bench, President Bill Clinton named Ruth Bader Ginsburg his pick for the first Democratic president's appointment to the Supreme Court in twenty-six years. Dubbed "the Thurgood Marshall of gender equality law," she was confirmed by the Senate ninety-seven to three and sworn in on August 10, 1993—the second woman ever to hold the office.